Heaven Right Now

Prophet Chronicles

By

Melvin Abercrombie, the Prophet.

Order this book online at www.trafford.com
or email orders@trafford.com

Most Trafford titles are also available at major online book retailers.

Printed in Victoria, BC, Canada.

ISBN: 978-1-4269-3204-5 (sc)

ISBN: 978-1-4269-3206-9 (e-book)

Library of Congress Control Number: 2010906375

*Our mission is to efficiently provide the world's finest, most comprehensive book publishing
service, enabling every author to experience success. To find out how to publish your
book, your way, and have it available worldwide, visit us online at www.trafford.com*

Trafford rev. 4/30/2010

www.trafford.com

North America & international
toll-free: 1 888 232 4444 (USA & Canada)
phone: 250 383 6864 ♦ fax: 812 355 4082

CONTENTS

Chapter 1   1

Chapter 2   9

Chapter 3   17

Chapter 4   29

Chapter 5   39

Chapter 6   47

Chapter 7   53

Chapter 8   63

Chapter 9   69

Chapter 10   73

Chapter 11   85

CHAPTER 1

I AM THE PROPHET.I AM THE WATCHER. NOW AFTER
OVER 2,000 YEARS I CAN PROCLAIM I AM A VAMPIRE.I
LONGED FOR THIS DAY WHEN THE WORLD WOULD BE
READY TO KNOW THE TRUTH.I HAVE LIVED MANY
LIFETIMES.MY SOUL IS IMMORTAL,ALTHOUGH I MUST
GO INTO THIS TEMPORARY BODY,TO FEED,EAT AND
DRINK.THE CURSE PUT ON US BECAUSE OF OUR SIN WE
MUST BEAR. WE HAVE KEPT OUR SECRET AND WE HAVE
KEPT THE LAW "TO KNOW,TO DARE,TO REMAIN SILENT".
NOW IT IS TIME TO COME OUT OF THE PROVERBIAL
CLOSET AND EXPOSE ALL THE FALSE SO CALLED
VAMPIRES.YES, THEY WILL ATTACK ME,THEY WILL DENY
AND TRY TO IGNORE THIS BOOK. A REAL VAMPIRE DOES
NOT DRINK BLOOD,THIS IS ABSURD BUT WE NEEDED
TO HIDE THE TRUTH THRU THE YEARS SO WE WOULD
NOT GO THRU WHAT OUR SISTERS, THE WITCHES,

WENT THRU. WE ABSORB YOUR POWER/ENERGY AND THRIVE ON IT.THAT IS HOW WE SURVIVE.I CAN TOUCH YOU OR MERELY SHAKE YOUR HAND AND ABSORB YOUR ENERGY. USING MY FIVE SENSES OF TOUCH,TASTE,SMELL,SEE AND HEAR I CAN ABSORB YOUR ENERGY THRU MY EYES,WHEN I SEE YOU, MY EYES ARE ACTUALLY TOUCHING YOU AND JUST LIKE A VACUUM CLEANER I CAN ABSORB YOUR ENERGY. I CAN HEAR YOU ON A TELEPHONE ALL ACROSS EUROPE AND THE MOMENT MY EARS HEAR YOUR VOICE I AM TOUCHING YOU THRU MY HEARING. DOES THIS AMUSE YOU? ARE YOU LAUGHING? GO AHEAD AND LAUGH AS I DRAIN YOUR ENERGY AND YOU WONDER WHY AFTER ALL DAY YOU ARE SO TIRED. WHERE DID ALL THE ENERGY GO? YOU HAVE TO EAT AND DRINK TO MAKE YOUR BODY CREATE MORE ENERGY. THE FOOD YOU EAT AS IT GOES THRU YOUR DIGESTIVE TRACT WILL CONVERT THE SIMPLE FOOD TO ENERGY.IF YOU ARE ONE OF THOSE BIBLE THUMPERS THEN SO AM I, THEN READ THE STORY ABOUT THE WOMAN WHO HAD THE PROBLEM OF BLEEDING AND THE ISSUE OF BLOOD WHO KNEW IF SHE COULD ONLY TOUCH THE HEM OF THE CHRIST GARMENT SHE COULD BE HEALED. THEY WERE IN A CROWD AND JESUS KNEW SOMEONE TOUCHED HIM AND TOOK SOME OF HIS POWER.THIS IS HOW THE SON OF GOD HAS THE POWER TO HEAL BY LAYING ON OF HANDS.HE SIMPLY DRAWS POWER FROM THE CROWD AND DRAWS IT INTO THE PERSON NEEDING THE HEALING, AS A MINISTER I HAVE DONE THIS THOUSANDS OF TIMES. IN A WAY THIS BOOK IS A RELIGIOUS BOOK BUT WHEN YOU REALIZE 90% OF THE PEOPLE IN THIS WORLD ARE GOING ABOUT IT WRONG, THEN A TIME HAS TO COME TO SHOW THE TRUTH. IT IS UP TO YOU, AS A INDIVIDUAL ,TO READ THIS, ACCEPT IT OR IGNORE IT BUT WITH A OPEN MIND IMAGINE WHAT IF ALL THE THINGS I AM SAYING ARE THE TRUTH? REMEMBER I AM THE PROPHET, I AM THE VAMPIRE,I AM THE WATCHER. I AM WATCHING YOU. THIS WILL BE THE

FIRST CHAPTER OF HEAVEN, RIGHT NOW. WHAT IF I TELL YOU THAT YOU ARE LIVING IN YOUR HEAVEN/HELL RIGHT NOW? WOULD YOU THINK I AM CRAZY? IF YOU STOP AND THINK ABOUT THIS PLACE CALLED HEAVEN AND WHAT DIFFERENT SO CALLED RELIGIONS DESCRIBE IT WILL BE LIKE. THEN WITH A OPEN MIND IMAGINE AFTER YOU LIVED THIS 40,60,80 PLUS YEARS YOU DO ACTUALLY DIE THEN YOU HOPE YOU WILL EITHER GET TO GO TO HEAVEN OR BURN IN HELL FOREVER AND EVER. DOES THAT MAKE SENSE? SO WHAT ABOUT THE LAST 40,60,80 YEARS? ARE THEY JUST WASTED? DO THEY ACCOUNT FOR ANYTHING? SOME OF THE TOPICS I WILL DISCUSS WILL BE REPEATED IN VARIOUS CHAPTERS,SOME THINGS NEED TO BE REPEATED. THE AVERAGE HUMAN WILL ONLY REMEMBER 20% OF WHAT THEY READ, SO I ASK YOU TO GET YOUR MONEY WORTH BY READING THIS OVER AND OVER. SO,ON THE OTHER HAND,IMAGINE YOU WASTED THIS LIFE AND NOW YOU ARE DEAD SO WHAT WILL IT BE LIKE IN HEAVEN? DO YOU GET TO LAY AROUND ALL DAY PLAYING A HARP? DO YOU EAT? DRINK? HOW OLD WILL YOU BE? CAN YOU GET MARRIED? HAVE SEX AND CHILDREN? DO YOU GET 20 VIRGINS LIKE THE ISLAM BELIEVE? WHAT WILL YOU DO WITH 20 VIRGINS ANYWAY? SURE IT WILL BE FUN FOR AWHILE BUT AFTER A WHILE THEY WILL NO LONGER BE VIRGINS BUT NOW YOU HAVE 20 WIVES WHICH ARE ALL PREGNANT AND THEN YOU HAVE 20 LITTLE BABIES,ONE STARTS CRYING AND WAKES THE OTHERS SO NOW YOU HAVE 20 DIRTY DIAPERS AND A WHOLE LOT OF WASHING,THEN OF COURSE YOU HAVE 20 JEALOUS WOMAN SAYING YOU LOVE HER MORE THEN ME AND ALL WANTING YOU TO SPEND TIME WITH THEM,SO DO YOU ALL SLEEP TOGETHER OR HAVE TURNS? WHAT STARTS OUT AS SOMETHING EXCITING THEN "WHEN THE HONEYMOON IS OVER" OR RATHER 20 HONEYMOONS ARE OVER AFTER 20 WEDDINGS ARE OVER. YOU ARE GOING TO NEED A BIG MANSION BUT DON'T WORRY JESUS SAID HE WILL BUILD YOU A

MANSION. SO IS JESUS GOING TO BUY ALL YOUR FOOD? IS JESUS GOING TO PROVIDE ALL YOUR CLOTHES? DIAMOND WEDDING RINGS FOR ALL THE WOMAN? DOES THE GROOM HAVE 20 WEDDING RINGS? WHO PAYS THE ELECTRIC BILL? A HOUSE THIS BIG WITH AT LEAST 21 BEDROOMS,ONE FOR EACH WIFE AND THE GROOM HAS TO HAVE A SEPARATE CHAMBER FOR HIS SELF THEN IF THEY HAVE CHILDREN DO YOU PILE ALL THEM IN ONE ROOM OR DO THEY GET THEIR OWN BEDROOM TOO? SO IMAGINE THE AIR CONDITIONING AND HEATING BILL PLUS WATER,SEWER HOW MANY BATHROOMS? DO THEY WAIT IN LINE OR DO THEY EACH HAVE THEIR OWN BATHROOM? IF THEY EAT AND DRINK THEY WILL NEED A LOT OF BATHROOMS SO WHO WILL KILL THE COW,CHICKEN,TURKEY? WHO GROWS THE VEGETABLES? WILL THEIR BE GROCERY STORES AND WAL-MARTS? WILL WE HAVE MONEY?IF SO WILL IT BE AMERICAN?PESOS?YEN? WHAT LANGUAGE WILL WE SPEAK? DO WE PUSH ONE FOR ENGLISH? TWO FOR SPANISH? WHAT DO WE PUSH FOR GERMAN? OR FRENCH? OR ITALIAN? SO,ON THE OTHER HAND IF YOU ACCEPT THE IDEA OF RE-INCARNATION THEN EVERYTHING SORT OF MAKES SENSE.THE LIFE YOU ARE LIVING RIGHT NOW IS WHAT YOU HAVE CREATED FROM YOUR PAST LIFE. IF YOU ARE RICH OR POOR,HEALTHY OR SICK COULD IT BE BECAUSE OF THINGS YOU DONE IN YOUR PAST LIFE? REMEMBER ONE LIFE YOU MAY BE A WHITE MALE BUT IN A PAST LIFE YOU COULD HAVE BEEN A BLACK FEMALE.ONE LIFE YOU COULD BE BORN IN AMERICA,ONE LIFE YOU COULD BE BORN IN RUSSIA.SO A DIFFERENT CULTURE,DIFFERENT LANGUAGE,DIFFERENT LIFE STYLE. EVERY LIFE YOU LIVE YOU HAVE TO EXPERIENCE CERTAIN THINGS,WHY? WHAT ARE YOU LIVING FOR? WHY ARE YOU HERE NOW?? WHAT PURPOSE ARE YOU HERE? WHAT DO YOU NEED TO EXPERIENCE? HOW DO YOU KNOW WHAT ITS LIKE TO BE BORN BLIND UNLESS YOU ACTUALLY EXPERIENCE IT? WHAT IS THE DIFFERENCE IN BEING BORN BLIND

AND BEING BORN, ABLE TO SEE, THEN GO BLIND? WILL YOU SEE THINGS FROM A DIFFERENT PROSPECTIVE? AT LEAST IF YOU CAN SEE, THEN GO BLIND, YOU AT LEAST KNOW WHAT A HUMAN LOOKS LIKE, WHAT A ELEPHANT ,TREE,HOUSE,BOAT,AIRPLANE ETC. LOOKS LIKE. CAN YOU IMAGINE TRYING TO TELL SOMEONE WHO WAS BORN BLIND WHAT ALL THESE THINGS LOOK LIKE? ITS THE SAME WITH DEAF OR SOME CRIPPLING DISEASE. HOW DO YOU KNOW WHAT ITS LIKE UNTIL YOU "WALK A MILE IN THEIR SHOES". SO CAN YOU DO ALL THESE THINGS IN ONE LIFETIME? CAN YOU EXPERIENCE ALL THESE THINGS IN ONE LIFE TIME? I KNOW AS A VAMPIRE,I HAVE LIVED MANY LIVES,ONE WAS A PIRATE. I WAS NOBODY FAMOUS,ALL MY FAMILY DIED FROM THIS DISEASE,I WAS SPARED,WHY? BECAUSE OF MY POWER,YES JUST LIKE YOU I DO DIE BUT ONLY FROM THIS PHYSICAL BODY . MY MENTAL AND SPIRITUAL BODY GOES INTO THE NEXT LIFE.SOME OF MY PAST LIFES I DO REMEMBER OTHERS I CHOOSE NOT TO. WHEN YOU LIVE BY THE SWORD THEN YOU WILL DIE BY THE SWORD.WHEN ALL MY FAMILY DIED I CHOSE TO DRINK AWAY MY PROBLEMS THRU A BOTTLE OF RUM. ONE DAY I WOKE UP ON A SHIP FAR FROM LAND. I HAD TWO CHOICES JUMP OVER BOARD OR SURVIVE.I REMEMBER OUR FIRST BATTLE A MAN WAS RUNNING TOWARDS ME WITH A SWORD IN HIS HAND. I HAD A CHOICE TO DEFEND MY SELF OR LET HIM KILL ME. I KNEW IF I LEFT THIS BODY I WOULD ONLY GO INTO ANOTHER ONE BUT I ALSO KNEW I WAS RESPONSIBLE AND ACCOUNTABLE FOR MY ACTIONS. I WAS NOT READY TO MEET MY MAKER,MY CREATOR AND BE JUDGED FOR WHAT I HAVE DONE SO IT BECAME EASIER. MY SIMPLE LOGIC WAS TO SURVIVE. WHEN THIS BODY GETS OLD I WILL HAVE TIME TO ASK FOR FORGIVENESS AND GET TO GO TO HEAVEN.AT THE TIME MY RELIGION TAUGHT THAT THEIR WAS ONLY ONE LIFE,ONE CHANCE TO DO EVERYTHING, YOU EITHER GO TO HEAVEN OR BURN IN HELL FOREVER AND EVER. SO IF THIS IS HEAVEN RIGHT NOW ON THIS EARTH

THEN WHERE IS MY MANSIONS? DID YOU BUILD IT? WE,AS A SOCIETY, CREATED THIS LAZY WORLD, DON'T WORRY, JUST LAY AROUND AND DO NOTHING, THE GOVERNMENT WILL TAKE CARE OF YOU. IF YOU DON'T WANT TO WORK,JUST LAY AROUND AND YOU CAN GET GOVERNMENT HELP, THRU FOOD STAMPS,WELFARE AND GOVERNMENT ASSISTED HOUSING. SO ASK THIS GOVERNMENT TO BUILD YOU A MANSION, SO IF YOU HAVE 20 VIRGINS WHICH BECOME YOUR 20 WIVES I AM SURE THE GOVERNMENT WILL HELP GIVE YOU A PLACE OF YOUR OWN.BUT NOW IF YOU ARE IN HEAVEN THEN THE GOVERNMENT BECOMES GOD.ITS AMAZING, THEY BOTH START OFF WITH THE SAME FIRST TWO LETTERS GO. SO NOW WE HAVE THIS SOCIETY OF CO-DEPENDENT PEOPLE DEPENDING ON THE NEW " GO" ITS ALSO AMAZING THAT THE UNITED STATES ARE ONLY A FEW OF THIS WORLD THAT ACTUALLY GOES TO THIS EXTREME AS FAR AS ACCEPTING ANYONE,ANYWHERE AND GIVING THEM THIS FREEDOM, "COME ONE COME ALL TO AMERICA,LAND OF THE FREE,HOME OF THE BRAVE,ONE NATION UNDER GOD WITH LIBERTY JUSTICE FOR ALL". SO WE CAN ONLY IMAGINE THAT HEAVEN WILL BE LIKE AMERICA,RIGHT? SO IS GOD THE PRESIDENT? CAN WE VOTE HIM OUT? WHAT IF WE DON'T LIKE IT AND WANT SOMETHING ELSE? IS THAT WHAT HAPPENED ORIGINALLY WHEN THE THIRD OF THE ANGELS WERE CAST OUT OF HEAVEN? WHAT DID HAPPEN? WHY WOULD A THIRD OF ALL THE ANGELS REBEL? HOW MANY WERE THE THIRD? A THIRD OF 100? A THIRD OF A THOUSAND? THE WONDERFUL THING ABOUT CREATION IS WE ARE CREATED IN THE IMAGE OF OUR CREATORS. MY FIRST BOOK I WROTE I ASKED THE QUESTION "DOES GOD HAVE A PENIS?" BY MELVIN ABERCROMBIE UNDER TRAFFORD PUBLISHING. THIS WAS A QUESTION A TYPICAL 10 YEAR OLD WOULD ASK,ACTUALLY THE BOOK HAS 14 CHAPTERS EACH ASKING A QUESTION. MY SECOND BOOK "HARMONY,THE GREATEST STORY NEVER TOLD" BY MELVIN ABERCROMBIE

UNDER TRAFFORD PUBLISHING HAS THE SAME 14
CHAPTERS AND GOES MORE INTO THE FEMALE SIDE OF
GOD AND AT THE TIME SOME OF MY BELIEFS. THRU THE
YEARS I HAVE CHANGED AND MY RELIGIOUS BELIEFS
HAVE CHANGED TO, SO I HOPE AS YOU READ THIS,
THINK ABOUT THE SIX MILLION DOLLAR QUESTION,
WHAT IF I AM RIGHT? WHAT IF WE ARE ACTUALLY LIVING
THIS LIFE AND WE ARE ACTUALLY IN OUR VERSION OF
HEAVEN. WHEN WE DIE WE DO GO BEFORE OUR
CREATORS AND WE ARE JUDGED ACCORDING TO WHAT
WE DONE. IF WE DONE BAD,EVIL THINGS THEN WE DO
NOT GET TO HELP DECIDE OUR NEXT LIFE,BUT ON THE
OTHER HAND IF WE BALANCED THE SCALES OF LIFE
AND DID GOOD THEN WE HAVE A SAY SO ABOUT WHAT
WE WANT TO EXPERIENCE NEXT. DO YOU WANT SOME
PEARLY GATES? WHY? WILL A GATE KEEP SOMEONE OUT?
IF WE HAVE STREETS OF GOLD WILL THEY BE SLIPPERY
WHEN IT RAINS? GOLD WILL TARNISH AFTER AWHILE
AND IS ACTUALLY A SOFT METAL I WOULD ACTUALL
PREFER STREETS OF CONCRETE MAYBE SOME BEAUTIFUL
WHITE MANSIONS WITH GREEK COLUMNS BUT LOOK
AROUND AND WE HAVE CASTLES AND BEAUTIFUL
MANSIONS ALL OVER THE PLACE. THIS WORLD WAS
ONCE A BEAUTIFUL PLACE UNTIL WE, AS A SOCIETY, ARE
SLOWLY DESTROYING IT. GIVE US ANOTHER 100 YEARS
AND WE WILL ONLY MAKE THIS WORLD WORSE. UNTIL
WE REALIZE THIS IS OUR HEAVEN AND WE ARE
ACCOUNTABLE AND RESPONSIBLE FOR WHAT WE DO.
WE ARE NOT SAVED BY GRACE THAT IS A FALSE DELUSION
THAT RELIGION IS CRAMMING DOWN YOUR THROAT.
GO AHEAD DO WHAT EVER YOU WANT, WORSHIP OUR
CREATORS ON WHAT EVER DAY YOU WANT TO AND EAT
WHAT EVER YOU WANT TO, DON'T WORRY YOU ARE
SAVED BY GRACE, ALL YOU HAVE TO DO IS SAY" GOD
FORGIVE ME", ITS OK TO GO OUT AND KILL TEN PEOPLE,
YOU ARE NOT ACCOUNTABLE AND YOU ARE NOT
RESPONSIBLE, RIGHT BEFORE YOU DIE JUST SAY GOD
FORGIVE ME AND YOU GET TO GO TO HEAVEN AND

SPEND PARADISE FOREVER.AS A PIRATE THIS WAS MY RELIGIOUS BELIEF,WHEN THE SHIP I WAS ON FINALLY SANK IT WAS EVERYMAN FOR HIS SELF,THEIR WAS A LARGE PIECE OF WOOD FLOATING AND I SWAM TOWARDS IT AND CLIMBED ON.I FELL ASLEEP AND WOKE THE NEXT MORNING,HUNGARY,THIRSTY AND NO ONE AROUND,IF ANYONE DID SURVIVE THEY WERE LONG GONE. NOTHING BUT WATER AS FAR AS I COULD SEE. I DESERVED THIS. THE MEAN CRUEL THINGS I HAVE DONE, THEN THIS IS MY FATE. FOR THREE DAYS I FLOATED,I WAS DELIRIOUS AND STARTED LAUGHING TO MY SELF. HERE I AM SURROUNDED BY WATER AND I AM DYING OF THIRST. HERE I AM SURROUNDED BY ALL THIS FOOD AND I AM STARVING.I FINALLY DECIDED TO ACCEPT MY FATE AND ASK MY CREATORS,MY FATHER GOD AND MOTHER GODDESS TO FORGIVE ME. I ROLLED OFF THE BOARD, TO WEAK TO CLIMB BACK ON.I ACCEPTED MY FATE,WHAT EVER MY NEXT LIFE WILL BE I WILL ACCEPT IT, THEN A WOMAN CAME UP BEHIND ME WITH LONG BLONDE HAIR AND BLUE EYES AND HELPED ME GET TO SHORE.WAS THIS ALL A DREAM? WAS THIS MY GUARDIAN ANGEL? WAS THIS A MERMAID? I ONLY REMEMBER MY FEET TOUCHING THE SANDY SHORE AND WHEN I LOOKED BACK SHE WAS GONE. WHY WAS I SPARED? IN MY LAST FEW MOMENTS IN AGONY,DID SOME ONE REALLY HEAR MY VOICE? I KNEW I HAD TO CHANGE MY WAYS.THE REST OF THIS LIFE AND MY NEXT LIFE WILL BE TO HELP OTHERS. YES I AM A VAMPYRE, I AM TEMPORARY STUCK IN THIS MORTAL BODY,ONLY TO FEED AND SURVIVE. THE SUN IT DOESN'T BOTHER ME,MOST OF OUR KINDRED SPIRITS LOVE TO DO THEIR WORK BEHIND THE VEIL OF DARKNESS. I AM A MORNING PERSON.I WROTE SOME POEM'S UNDER WWW.POETRY.COM AND UNDER MY NAME DURING THIS LIFETIME WHICH IS MELVIN ABERCROMBIE SO GO TO THE WEBSITE,ITS FREE,MY GIFT TO YOU.

CHAPTER 2

THIS WILL BE THE SECOND CHAPTER . ONE OF MY POEMS TALK ABOUT THE FACT THAT I WAS THERE WHEN THEY NAILED HIM TO THE CROSS. I WAS NOBODY SPECIAL BUT AS A VAMPYRE, I LIVED MANY LIFE'S AND KNEW THIS PERSON WAS SPECIAL.I KNEW HE HAD THE POWER,TEN TIMES THE POWER OF ANY OTHER PERSON.I ALSO LEARNED THE HEBREW LANGUAGE AND CONCEALED MY SELF AS A TRUE HEBREW,IN REALITY I WAS A UNCIRCUMCISED GENTILE,WE WILL TALK ABOUT THIS IN ANOTHER CHAPTER BUT FOR NOW I WANTED TO GET CLOSER TO THIS GOD CALLED YAHWEH AND THIS GODDESS WHO WAS KNOWN AS THE SHEKINAH. MOSTLY I WANTED TO GET CLOSER TO THIS MAN WHO CALLS HIM SELF THE "SON OF GOD," ARE WE NOT ALL THE SONS AND DAUGHTERS OF OUR GOD AND GODDESS? THEY TAUGHT THE PEOPLE TO KEEP THE LAWS,AND

COMMANDMENTS,NOT JUST TEN BUT ALL 613, OUR LAW WAS "TO KNOW,TO DARE,TO REMAIN SILENT". WE ALSO FOLLOWED THE WITCHES LAW , WHICH WERE OUR PAGAN SISTERS, WHO WORSHIPPED OUR MOTHER GODDESS AND THAT WAS "AND YOU HARM NONE, DO WHAT YOU WILL". SO DOES IT MATTER WHAT DAY WE WORSHIP OUR CREATORS? WE KNOW THIS HAS BEEN A TOPIC FOR THOUSANDS OF YEARS.WE CAN ARGUE TILL THE COWS COME HOME ABOUT WHY SO AND SO SAID IT DOES NOT MATTER AND WHAT SO AND SO SAID IN HIS BOOK. THE BOTTOM LINE TO ME WOULD BE "WHAT WOULD THE REAL JESUS(YAHSHUA) DO?" WHAT DAY DID THE REAL JESUS OBSERVE? WE KNOW DURING THE LAST LESSON THAT DURING THE 33 YEARS THAT JESUS WAS ON THIS EARTH THAT HE WAS A GOOD HEBREW/ JEWISH PERSON. THE NEW TESTAMENT WAS NOT EVEN CREATED UNTIL LONG AFTER HE DIED. WE DO KNOW THAT AROUND 313AD A ROMAN EMPERIOR NAMED CONSTANTINE COMBINED THE ORIGINAL 7TH DAY SAB-BATH WITH THE PAGAN 1ST DAY THAT WORSHIPPED THE SUN GOD TOGETHER AND DECLARED THAT JESUS DID AROSE ON THE FIRST DAY OF THE WEEK AND WE SHOULD ALL WORSHIP TOGETHER.I WAS THERE WHEN ALL THIS WAS HAPPENING AND KNEW DEEP DOWN THIS WILL BE TROUBLE. I WAS A ROMAN SOLDIER, JUST A PERSON WHO TRIED TO SURVIVE. I WAS A ROMAN SOL-DIER WHO DID HAVE SOME AUTHORITY. I HAD THREE WIVES WHICH WAS COMMON. OUR GOD WAS CALLED JUPITER AND OUR GODDESS WAS CALLED JUNO.IN SECRET I WOULD STILL FOLLOW THE HEBREW WHO CALLED THEIR MALE GOD YAHWEH AND THE FEMALE GODDESS THE SHEKINAH, I FELT MORE COMFORTABLE BUT KNEW THIS WAS A DEEP SECRET I HAD TO CONCEAL,JUST LIKE THE FACT I WAS A VAMPYRE WHO LIVED OFF THE ENERGY OF PEOPLE EVERYONE KNEW I HAD THIS SPECIAL POWER AND I GAINED THEIR RE-SPECT.THRU THE YEARS I RE-INCARNATED AS A SLAVE,AS A WOMAN AND AS A FOREIGNER, WHO SPOKE A STRANGE

LANGUAGE. AS A ROMAN SOLDIER I FINALLY HAD THE POWER TO GIVE LIFE OR TAKE LIFE,BUT ONLY AS THE EMPERIOR PLEASE.WE KNOW THIS STARTED THE ORIGINAL ROMAN CATHOLIC CHURCH AND NOW WE KNOW WHY MODERN DAY CHRISTIANS WORSHIP THE CHRIST ON SUNDAY,THE 1ST DAY OF THE WEEK. IS THIS WHAT OUR FATHER INTENDED? DID JESUS(YAHSHUA), DURING THE 33 YEARS THAT HE WAS ALIVE,DID HE EVER WORSHIP HIS FATHER ON SUNDAY,THE FIRST DAY OF THE WEEK? NO HOW DO I KNOW THAT? MATTHEW,THE FIRST BOOK OF THIS NEW TESTAMENT GOES IN GREAT DETAIL TO EXPLAIN IN CHAPTER ONE THE GENEOLOGY,LINEAGE OF THE CHRIST. THIS LETS EVERYONE KNOW THAT HE HAD ALL THE QUALIFICATIONS TO BE THE LONG LOOKED FOR MESSIAH. AS A GOOD HEBREW/JEWISH PERSON HE NATURALLY DID ALL THE SAME THINGS THAT ALL HEBREW/JEWISH PEOPLE DID. REMEMBER THERE WAS NO NEW TESTAMENT,PEOPLE WERE NOT SAVED BY GRACE. ALL THEY HAD WAS THE LAW, THE TORAH,THE TANAKH.JESUS (YAHSHUA) KEPT THE 613 LAWS,WHICH EQUALS THE TEN COMMANDMENTS OF MOSES. HE KEPT THE TRUE FRIDAY NIGHT AND ALL DAY SATURDAY 7TH DAY SABBATH JUST LIKE ALL HEBREW/JEWISH PEOPLE ARE STILL DOING. HE SPOKE THE HEBREW LANGUAGE,STUDIED THE KABBALAH AND WORSHIPPED AT THE SYNAGOGUE. ON HIS THIRTEENTH BIRTHDAY HE WENT THRU HIS BAR MITSVOT JUST LIKE ALL HEBREW/JEWISH BOYS AND GIRLS AND BECAME A GROWN UP ABLE TO MARRY AND GET A JOB.WE KNOW HE FOLLOWED IN HIS EARTHLY FATHERS (JOSEPH) FOOTSTEPS AND BECAME " THE SON OF A CARPENTER". THE MAIN QUESTION WE NEED TO ASK NOW IS, WHAT IF THE REAL JESUS WAS ALIVE,IN FLESH AND BLOOD TODAY, AND WE ASKED HIM TO GO WITH US TO YOUR TYPICAL BAPTIST,METHODIST,ETC. CHURCH ON SUNDAY, WOULD HE GO? NO WHY? WE KNOW DURING THE 33 YEARS HE WAS ALIVE HE NEVER ONCE WORSHIPPED HIS FATHER ON SUNDAY,THE FIRST DAY OF

THE WEEK. WE KNOW HE WAS A GOOD HEBREW/JEWISH TYPE PERSON. WE KNOW DURING THE TIME THAT JESUS WAS ALIVE THERE WAS NO SUNDAY WORSHIP,THIS DID NOT HAPPEN TILL 313AD WHICH WAS ALMOST THREE HUNDRED YEARS AFTER HE DIED.WE KNOW AS ALL GOOD HEBREW/JEWISH PEOPLE ALL THEY HAD WERE THE TEN COMMANDMENTS OF EXODUS CHAPTER 20. THIS WAS THE LAW. WAS JESUS UNDER THE LAW? OF COURSE. DID JESUS COME TO CHANGE THE LAW? NO READ ALL OF MATTHEW CHAPTER FIVE ESPECIALLY THE LAST PART. JESUS IS TELLING YOU THAT "HE DID NOT COME TO CHANGE THE LAW,NOT ONE DOTTING OF THE I OR CROSSING OF THE T AND ANYONE WHO DOES WILL BE LEAST IN HIS KINGDOM". I KNOW AS A FORMER CHRISTIAN/BAPTIST PREACHER,JUST LIKE A LOT OF OTHERS I EXPLAINED THAT PAUL SAID THIS IN SO AND SO AND PETER SAID THIS IN SO AND SO. THE BOTTOM LINE, AM I A FOLLOWER OF PAUL? OR PETER? NO I CAN CALL MY SELF A REAL CHRISTIAN AM I UNDER THE LAW? YES I CHOOSE TO BE. AM I SAVED BY GRACE? NO JESUS DID NOT DIE ON THE CROSS FOR MY SINS, WE ARE STILL RESPONSIBILE AND ACCOUNTABLE FOR OUR SINS. JESUS DIED ON THE CROSS TO DO AWAY WITH THE SACRIFI-CIAL LAW. REMEMBER DURING JESUS TIME ANYONE WHO COMMITS A SIN,THE PENALTY WAS DEATH SO THE RABBI CAME UP WITH THE IDEA TO FEED THE POOR TO OFFER A ANIMAL AS A ATONEMENT FOR YOUR SINS SO A SHEEP,CALF,ETC WAS OFFERED AND THEY WOULD PRAY TO OUR FATHER FOR FORGIVENESS.YOU WILL NOTICE AFTER JESUS DIED THE HEBREW/JEWISH PEOPLE DID DO AWAY WITH THIS ANIMAL SACRIFICE.DO THE TYPI-CAL HEBREW/JEWISH PERSON TODAY ACCEPT JESUS AS THE MESSIAH? NO WHEN THEY COMMIT A SIN THEY GO TO THE SYNAGOGUE AND TALK TO THE RABBI WHO PRAYS TO GOD BUT ARE THEY SAVED BY GRACE? NO THEY ARE STILL ACCOUNTABLE AND STILL RESPONSI-BLE AND STILL HAVE TO CORRECT THE WRONG THEY DONE BECAUSE THEY ARE STILL UNDER THE LAW.I DID

SAY I WOULD EXPLAIN ABOUT THE REASON WE NAMED OUR MINISTRY BROKEN WING. I REMEMBER A STORY ABOUT A GOOD SHEPHERD WHO HAD A HUNDRED SHEEP. WHEN ONE WOULD RUN AWAY THE SHEPHERD WOULD LEAVE THE 99 AND GO LOOKING FOR THE LOST SHEEP AND REJOICE WHEN HE FOUND IT. IF THE SHEEP KEPT ON RUNNING AWAY THEN THE SHEPHERD WOULD BREAK ONE OF ITS LEGS. IN PAIN, THE SHEEP WOULD CRY OUT AND THE SHEPHERD WOULD PICK UP THE RUN AWAY SHEEP AND CARRY IT AROUND. THE SHEEP,HOPEFULLY LEARNED HIS LESSON AND QUIT RUNNING AWAY.THERE ARE SEVERAL SONGS ONE BY MARTINA MCBRIDE THAT GOES LIKE THIS,"WITH A BROKEN WING,SHE STILL CARRIES HER DREAM AND YOU OUGHT TO SEE HER FLY." ANOTHER SONG SAYS " A BROKEN WING NEEDS TIME TO HEAL BEFORE A HEART CAN FLY" AND MY FAVORITE WAS A SONG ABOUT A MAN TO HIS FATHER THAT SAID " HE'S A ANGEL WITH NO HALO AND ONE WING IN THE FIRE".I KNOW I PAWNED MY HALO FOR A CASE OF BEER AND A BOTTLE OF WHIS-KEY. SO INSTEAD OF THE GOOD SHEPHERD BREAKING MY LEG OUR FATHER BROKE MY WINGS SO I COULD NOT FLY UP TO HEAVEN AND JUST LIKE THIS RUN AWAY SHEEP, I TO RAN FROM GOD. FOR SEVERAL YEARS,I LET MY HAIR GROW OUT,GOT TATTOO'S, DID ALL THE WILD THINGS A REBEL CHILD WOULD DO. I DRINKED WITH THE DEVIL AND EVERY ONE THINKS THE DEVIL IS A MAN BUT I DISAGREE,I KNOW I DANCED WITH THE DEVIL AND SLEPT WITH HER. JUST LIKE THE FORMER CHAPTER WHERE EVERYONE IS ON THIS CIRCULAR STAIRCASE, I WAS WAY UP HIGH ALMOST TO THE TOP AND HAD TO HAVE THIS NEAR DEATH ACCIDENT TO KNOCK ME DOWN TO THE BOTTOM TO STRAIGHTEN ME OUT. YES, I HIT THE BOTTOM,LOST EVERYTHING. IT TOOK THAT FOR ME TO OPEN MY EYES AND SEE WHAT I HAD BECOME.I SHOULD HAVE DIED THAT NIGHT.THE THINGS I DONE I DESERVED TO DIE, OUT OF DESPERA-TION I CRIED OUT,I WAS NOT READY TO DIE,I HAD SO

MUCH I WANTED TO DO,I HAD TO PROMISE MY GOD THAT I WOULD CHANGE. SO I WENT FROM ONE EXTREME TO ANOTHER.I WANTED TO KNOW ABOUT EVERYTHING. WHY DID MY OLDER BROTHER HAVE TO DIE? WHY DID MY MOM HAVE TO DIE? WHY DID MY SON HAVE TO DIE? A FATHER IS NOT SUPPOSED TO BURY HIS SON BUT THEN I REALIZED WHAT OUR FATHER IN HEAVEN HAD TO DO,JUST STAND THERE AND WATCH HIS OWN SON DIE ON THE CROSS KNOWING HE HAD THE POWER TO SEND A THOUSAND ANGELS DOWN TO RESCUE HIM. SOMETIMES I WONDER WHAT WOULD THIS WORLD BE LIKE IF GOD WOULD HAVE DONE THAT? WOULD THE WORLD BE ANY DIFFERENT? "WE HAVE EYES BUT DO NOT SEE,WE HAVE EARS BUT DO NOT HEAR." SO EACH CHAPTER I LIKE TO TELL A LITTLE STORY THE FIRST CHAPTER WAS ABOUT THE CIRCULAR STAIRS, CHAPTER TWO GOES LIKE THIS, ONE DAY THE DEVIL CAME INTO A CROWDED CHURCH,AS HE WALKED DOWN THE AISLE,PEOPLE LOOKED UP AND STARTED RUNNING,THE FURTHER DOWN HE WALKED MORE PEOPLE GOT UP AND TOOK OFF RUNNING,THE SONG LEADER AND PIANO PLAYER TOOK OFF AND FINALLY THE PREACHER HIM SELF TOOK OFF RUNNING.THE DEVIL STOOD AT THE PULPIT AND LOOKED AROUND, EVERYONE WAS GONE EXCEPT ONE OLD MAN ON THE THIRD ROW.THE DEVIL JUMPS UP AND DOWN AND SHOUTS "AS I WALK DOWN THE CHURCH AISLE EVERYONE RUN'S AWAY EVEN THE PREACHER HIM SELF TOOK OFF RUNNING, DO YOU KNOW WHO I AM?" YES REPLIED THE OLD MAN," I KNOW WHO YOU ARE AND I AM NOT AFRAID OF YOU,I WAS MARRIED TO YOUR SISTER FOR 30 YEARS." THIS IS THE TYPE OF PEOPLE I WANT TO SURROUND MYSELF WITH. PEOPLE WHO HAVE IN THE PAST DANCED,DRINK,SLEPT WITH THE DEVIL BUT NOW REALIZE THEY ARE NOT AFRAID OF HIM/HER.PEOPLE WHO HAVE THE POWER OF THE "REAL JESUS" WHO UNDERSTAND WHO THE REAL GOD IS, DID THE REAL GOD CHANGE? IF WE LIVE IN THE UNITED STATES ARE WE

UNDER THE LAW OF THE UNITED STATES? CAN WE RUN THAT RED LIGHT? OR RUN THAT STOP SIGN? HOW MANY LAWS ARE THEIR THAT WE ARE UNDER? WE GRIPE AND COMPLAIN SAYING THE OLD HEBREW/JEWISH PEOPLE HAD 613 LAWS AND WE CAN NOT BE UNDER THAT MANY LAWS BUT I WILL GUARANTEE YOU IF YOU TAKE ALL THE SIMPLE LAWS AND ADD THEM UP INDIVIDUALLY WHAT NUMBER WOULD YOU COME UP WITH? DID YOU KNOW THAT GOD TOLD MOSES THAT IF YOU ADD UP THE 6,1,AND 3 THEN YOU WOULD COME UP WITH THE TEN COMMANDMENTS AND IF YOU OBEY THE TEN COMMANDMENTS THEN YOU ARE BASICALLY KEEPING ALL 613 LAWS? SO OUR LAWS ABOUT RUNNING A RED LIGHT OR STOP SIGN WHERE ARE THEY AT UNDER THE TEN? WHAT ABOUT" DO UNTO OTHERS AS YOU WOULD HAVE THEM DO UNTO YOU",IS THIS PART OF THE LAW? WHEN YOU COME TO A STOP SIGN OR RED LIGHT DO YOU RESPECT THAT OTHER PERSON IN THE SAME WAY YOU WOULD WANT THAT PERSON TO RESPECT YOU? WHAT WOULD THE WORLD BE LIKE IF EVERYONE SAID WE ARE NOT UNDER ANY LAW WE CAN GO OUT AND KILL,STEAL ANYTHING WE WANT,ANY WAY WE ARE NO LONGER UNDER THE OLD LAW,"WE ARE SAVED BY GRACE". ANOTHER STORY WAS A VERY MEAN EVIL MAN KILLED A LOT OF PEOPLE,CUT THEM UP,POURED GAS ON THEM AND BURNED THEIR BODIES,THEN RIGHT BEFORE HE DIED HE CRIED OUT FOR FORGIVENESS,WILL HE GO TO HEAVEN? THEN ANOTHER MAN WHO WENT TO CHURCH REGULARY,GAVE HIS TITHES AND OFFERINGS ALL HIS LIFE, THEN LOST HIS JOB,OUT OF DESPERATION HE STOLE A LOAF OF BREAD TO FEED HIS FAMILY BUT DIED WITHOUT REPENTING, WILL HE BURN IN HELL FOREVER AND EVER? DOES THIS SOUND LIKE A MERCIFUL GOD?

CHAPTER 3

THIS WILL BE THE THIRD CHAPTER, THE LEVITICAL LAWS. DOES IT MATTER WHAT FOODS WE EAT? WHEN OUR GOD AND GODDESS CREATED THIS WORLD, THEY CREATED CERTAIN FOODS THEY DECLARED AS CLEAN AND UNCLEAN. SO THE NEXT QUESTION IS, IF THEY DID NOT WANT US TO EAT IT THEN WHY DID THEY CREATE IT? I AM SURE WHEN THE DESIGN OF THIS WORLD WAS THOUGHT OF THEN THEY KNEW THERE WOULD BE WASTE. EVERYTHING MUST LIVE FOR SO LONG, THEN DIE. THIS IS THE LIFE CYCLE.JUST LIKE ME, AS A VAMPIRE, I MUST GO INTO ANOTHER PHYSICAL BODY. KNOWING IT WILL BE TEMPORARY BUT ALSO KNOWING I HAVE A IMMORTAL SOUL,SOMETIMES I WISH THIS WOULD JUST END AND EACH LIFETIME I PRAY TO OUR YAHWEH AND SHEKINAH TO JUST LET ME REST AND SOMETIMES I DO JUST GO TO THIS OTHER PLACE FOR

AWHILE. ITS NOT WHAT YOU WOULD CALL HEAVEN OR HELL. JUST A QUITE PEACEFUL PLACE WHERE I DO NOT HAVE TO EAT OR DRINK. JUST LIKE SOME ONE WHO WENT TO SLEEP FOR SEVERAL HUNDRED YEARS, THEN AWOKE.I HAVE NO PHYSICAL BODY BUT NOW I AWAKE AND I AM HUNGRY AND THIRSTY, SO I CALL UPON MY YAHWEH AND MY SHEKINAH TO LET ME GO INTO AN-OTHER LIFE.THEN REALIZE THE WORLD HAS CHANGED,THE SLEEP DID ME GOOD,YES I DID NEED THE REST. SO WHEN SOMETHING DIES WHERE DOES IT GO? IF LEFT ALONE WHAT EVER DIES WILL EVENTUALLY ROT AWAY AND GO BACK TO EARTH,FROM WHERE IT CAME. ASHES TO ASHES,DUST TO DUST.BY CREATING CERTAIN ANIMALS,FISH AND BIRDS TO BE SCAVENGER THEN THIS WILL SPEED UP THIS PROCESS. THE PEOPLE WHO WROTE THE DIFFERENT BOOKS OF THE BIBLE FELT INSPIRED BY SOME HIGHER POWER TO PUT DOWN IN WRITING SOME OF THE IDEAS THAT MADE SENSE AT THE TIME. WE DO KNOW EVEN TODAY,AFTER THOU-SANDS OF YEARS THAT ISLAM,JEWISH AND SOME CHRIS-TIANS TRY TO KEEP THE KOSHER FOOD LAWS. SOME PEOPLE WHO ARE ATHEIST OR EVOLUTIONIST,WHO DO NOT BELIEVE IN ANY KIND OF GOD OR GODDESS STILL KEEP THE KOSHER FOOD LAW BECAUSE IT MAKES SENSE. THE BIBLE CLEARLY TELLS US THAT PORK IS A SCAVEN-GER FOOD. WE KNOW THAT THERE IS A BACTERIA IN PORK THAT IF EATEN CAN GROW IN YOU. COULD THIS BE WHY SOME PEOPLE HAVE SOME DISEASE'S? EVEN IF YOU COOK PORK TO A HIGHER TEMPERATURE TO KILL THIS BACTERIA DOES THE BACTERIA JUST GO AWAY? DOES THE BACTERIA JUST DISAPEAR? IF YOU EAT THIS PORK THEN YOU ARE EATING THIS DEAD BACTERIA OR HOPE IT ALL IS DEAD. ITS THE SAME WAY WITH FISH THE ONLY CLEAN KOSHER FOOD FROM THE WATER WILL HAVE FINS AND SCALES. WE KNOW CATFISH HAS FINS BUT NO SCALES.WE ALSO KNOW TO CATCH CATFISH YOU HAVE TO FISH FROM THE BOTTOM OF THE WATER BECAUSE THAT IS WHERE THEY STAY,THEY ARE BOTTOM

FEEDERS, EATING THE DEAD FISH. THE SAME WITH SHRIMP AND LOBSTER,IF YOU LOOK AT WHAT THESE EAT THEN YOU BECOME WHAT YOU EAT. THERE IS A OLD SAYING YOU ARE WHAT YOU EAT. IF YOU EAT FAT GREASY FOODS THEN YOU BECOME A FAT GREASY PERSON. IF YOU EAT LEAN, HEALTHY FOODS THEN YOU BECOME A LEAN, HEALTHY PERSON,AGAIN YOU ARE WHAT YOU EAT. YOU CAN HAVE ALL THE DIET PLANS IN THE WORLD. THEY DO NOT WORK BECAUSE THE AVER-AGE PERSON USES ONE OF THE 7 DEADLY SINS CALLED GREED. ANYTHING IN MODERATION IS NORMAL,YOUR BODY WILL TELL YOU THAT YOU ARE FULL,BUT YOU SEE MORE ON YOUR PLATE AND GREED KICKS IN.THE WORSE THING THAT SOCIETY CREATED IS "ALL YOU CAN EAT BUFFET" TYPE RESTURANTS. PEOPLE PAY MONEY TO GO IN AND THEY WANT A GOOD DEAL SO THEY KEEP ON EATING TO GET THEIR MONEY'S WORTH. MILLIONS AND MILLIONS OF DOLLARS ARE BEING SPENT ON DIET PLANS BUT EVERYONE DOES NOT WANT TO DO WHAT IT TAKES TO LOSE THE WEIGHT,WE WANT A MAGIC PILL THAT LETS US EAT ALL WE WANT AND STILL LOSE WEIGHT.THERE IS NO MAGIC PILL,AGAIN YOU ARE WHAT YOU EAT. IF YOU EAT A LITLLE IN MOD-ERATIONS THEN YOU WILL BE LITTLE,IF YOU ARE GREEDY AND STUFF YOUR SELF THEN YOU BECOME OVERWEIGHT. THIS DOES NOT HAPPEN OVER NIGHT AND LOSING WEIGHT IS NOT A OVER NIGHT SOLUTION. IF EVERY PERSON WOULD READ LEVITICUS IN THEIR BIBLES AND SIMPLY TRY TO DO THE MINIMUM OF WHAT THEY SHOULD DO THEN IMAGINE HOW MUCH BETTER YOU WOULD FEEL? SO THE BIG QUESTION IS "WHAT WOULD THE REAL JESUS DO?" IF JESUS WAS ALIVE AND YOU ASKED HIM TO GO WITH YOU TO RED LOBSTER AND EAT WOULD HE GO? NO IF YOU ASKED JESUS TO GO WITH YOU TO THIS "ALL YOU CAN EAT CATFISH BUFFET" WOULD HE GO? NO HOW DO I KNOW THIS? BY READ-ING THE BIBLE I KNOW THAT JESUS WAS A GOOD HEBREW/JEWISH TYPE PERSON. REMEMBER THE NEW

TESTAMENT WAS NOT CREATED YET. THE PEOPLE WHO CREATED THE NEW TESTAMENT WAITED UNTIL LONG AFTER JESUS DIED THEN IN 49AD MARK WAS THE FIRST TO WRITE HIS VERSION OF WHAT HAPPENED,SO IF JESUS WAS 33 YEARS OLD THEN THERE WAS A TIME PERIOD OF APPROXIMATELY 15 YEARS BEFORE ANY BOOK WAS WRITTEN. SO WHAT HAPPENED DURING THIS "LOST " 15 YEARS? MORE THEN LIKELY THE 12 DISCIPLES WERE SCATTERED AND AFRAID TO BE PUNISHED THE SAME WAY. THEY KNEW THEY HAD TO KEEP THE TEACHINGS AND THEY FELT THAT JESUS(YAHSHUA) WAS THE TRUE "SON OF GOD" THEY ACTUALLY THOUGHT THAT JESUS WOULD CALL UPON THIS "LEGION OF ANGELS" TO COME RESCUE HIM AT THE LAST MINUTE.THIS IS WHY JUDAS TURNED HIM IN. JUDAS DID NOT BETRAY HIM,JUDAS KNEW WHO HE WAS AND FELT THAT THE ANGELS WOULD COME AT THE LAST MINUTE THEN THE WORLD WOULD KNOW. ALL OF THE TEACHINGS OF JESUS LED UP TO THIS SACRIFICE. JESUS DID NOT DIE ON THE CROSS FOR YOUR SINS,YOU ARE ACCOUNTABLE AND RESPONSIBLE FOR WHAT EVER YOU DO. JESUS(YAHSHUA) DIED ON THE CROSS TO DO AWAY WITH THIS SACRIFICIAL LAW.UP TO THIS TIME ANY HEBREW/JEWISH PERSON WHO COMMITED A SIN COULD GO TO THE SYNOGUE AND TALK TO THE RABBI,HE WOULD TELL THEM WHAT ANIMAL TO BUY WHETHER ITS A CALF,SHEEP OR OTHER ANIMAL AND THAT ANIMAL WOULD BE SACRIFICED FOR YOUR SINS. THE RABBI WOULD USE THIS TO FEED THE HOMELESS AND POOR SO THERE WAS A GOOD OUTCOME.THE CHRISTIANS WHO SAY THAT THERE IS ONLY A MALE GOD,A MALE SON OF GOD AND A MALE HOLY SPIRIT BUT THEY ARE ALL ONE GOD, THEN WHEN JESUS DIED ON THE CROSS WHO DID HE CRY OUT TO? IF YOU GET TO HEAVEN AND THERE IS ONLY ONE GOD THEN WHO IS ON THE RIGHT SIDE? THE HEBREW/JEWISH PEOPLE HAVE 613 LAWS AND WE,AS CHRISTIANS FEEL WE CAN NOT BE UNDER THAT MANY LAWS BUT IF YOU ASK ANY

LAWYER TO WRITE OUT ALL THE LAWS OF THE UNITED STATES THEN YOU WILL PROBABLY FIND A LOT MORE. THE REAL SIMPLE ANSWER IS SIMPLE ARITHMETIC IF YOU ADD THE 613 LAWS TO BE 6+1+3 THEN YOU WILL HAVE THE 10 COMMANDMENTS WHICH NO ONE WANTS TO KEEP THEM,ESPECIALLY COMMANDMENT NUMBER FOUR WHICH ARE IN EXODUS CHAPTER 20 BUT THEN IF YOU TAKE THE SIMPLE 10 COMMANMENTS AND ADD 1+0 AND YOU GET ONE. WHAT IS THE ONE LAW? EVERYONE KNOWS THE GOLDEN RULE " DO UNTO OTHERS AS YOU WOULD HAVE THEM TO DO UNTO YOU." YOU DON'T WANT SOMEONE TO KILL YOU,DO YOU? OF COURSE NOT BUT WHAT GIVES YOU THE RIGHT TO KILL SOMEONE THEN EXPECT NOT THE SAME? YOU CAN KILL SOMEONE,GO TO JAIL A FEW YEARS THEN GET AWAY. IS THIS FAIR? DID YOU ACTUALLY GET AWAY WITH THIS? REMEMBER WHEN YOU DO DIE,YOUR BODY WILL GO BACK TO MOTHER EARTH FROM WHICH IT CAME, YOUR SPIRIT/SOUL WILL GO TO HEAVEN AND BE JUDGED. "EVERY KNEE SHALL BOW AND EVERY TONGUE SHALL CONFESS". DO YOU GET TO STAY UP THERE IN HEAVEN? AGAIN WHAT DO YOU DO UP THERE? CAN YOU EAT? DRINK? HOW OLD WILL YOU BE? CAN YOU GET MARRIED? HAVE SEX? CREATE BABIES? IF YOU USE COMMON SENSE THEN YOU HAVE NOT DONE ALL THE THINGS YOU NEED TO DO DURING ONE LIFETIME.COMMON SENSE WOULD TELL YOU THAT YOU NEED AND WANT TO EXPERIENCE MORE THINGS. HOW DO YOU KNOW WHAT ITS LIKE TO BE BLIND UNLESS YOU LIVE A LIFE AND EXPERIENCE THIS? ONE CASE WOULD BE IF YOU WERE BORN AND COULD SEE THEN BECOME BLIND THEN AT LEAST YOU WOULD HAVE A MEMORY OF WHAT A HUMAN LOOKS LIKE. WHAT A ELEPHANT,GIRA FFE,OCTUPUS,COW,DOG,BIRD,ETC LOOKS LIKE. WOULD A PERSON WHO WAS BORN BLIND HAVE A DIFFERENT EXPERIENCE ABOUT WHAT A ELEPANT,COW,OCTAPUS,BIRD WOULD LOOK LIKE? SAME WITH HEARING WOULD A PERSON WHO COULD

HEAR AND GO DEAF HAVE A DIFFERENT EXPERIENCE THEN SOME ONE WHO WAS BORN DEAF AND NEVER HEARING THE SIMPLE PIANO? EVERY LIFE WE LIVE WE WILL EXPERIENCE DIFFERENT THINGS,WOULD IT BE FAIR TO SAY YOU ONLY GET ONE CHANCE IN LIFE AND THAT IS IT? THEN EVERYONE EITHER GETS TO GO TO HEAVEN FOR EVER AND EVER OR YOU WILL BURN IN HELL FOR EVER AND EVER? DOES THIS SOUND FAIR TO YOU? THE MAJORITY OF PEOPLE WHO THINK THEY ARE CHRISTIAN MEAN WELL THEY HAVE GOOD INTEN- TIONS BUT "ON THE OTHER HAND" THEY HAVE BEEN MIS-LEAD.ONE OF US IS WRONG,IF I AM WRONG SHOW ME WHERE I AM WRONG.MY COMMON SENSE AND GOOD OLD GUT FEELINGS TELL ME THEIR HAS TO BE MORE TO LIFE. WHERE DID THIS IDEA ABOUT RE-IN- CARNATION COME FROM? IF, IN THE BEGINNING ADAM AND EVE KNEW THERE WAS ONLY ONE CHANCE THEN THIS WOULD BE PASSED DOWN,GENERATION AFTER GENERATION, THE SAME AS THE FEMALE SIDE OF GOD WHERE DID WE COME UP WITH THIS IDEA OF RE-IN- CARNATION AND A FEMALE SIDE OF GOD? THRU THE YEARS GENERATIONS WOULD TELL THE NEXT GENER- ATION, REMEMBER THEY DID NOT HAVE PRINTING MACHINES,XEROX PAPER,TELEPHONES,TELEVISION,RA DIO,CAMERA'S,AIRPLANES,REFRIGERATORS,MICROWA VES,CARS AND MOTORCYCLES.SOME PEOPLE WOULD SAY IF JESUS WAS ALIVE TODAY HE WOULD NOT RIDE AROUND ON A DONKEY HE WOULD RIDE A MOTORCY- CLE BECAUSE HE COULD GET AROUND EASY.I RIDE A HARLEY DAVIDSON DYNA SUPERGLIDE AND I WOULD LIKE TO THINK MAYBE JESUS WOULD RIDE A HARLEY WITH HIS LONG HAIR AND BEARD MOST CHURCH'S WOULD NOT ALLOW HIM IN THEIR CHURCH IF HE DROVE UP ON A MOTORCYCLE.THERE WAS A STORY ABOUT THIS MAN WHO HAD HOLES IN HIS PANTS AND SHIRT WENT TO A CHURCH AND THE PEOPLE LOOKED AT HIM AND DID NOT WANT TO TALK TO HIM. AFTER THE CHURCH SERVICE, THE PREACHER CAME DOWN

AND TOLD THE MAN "MAYBE YOU SHOULD TALK TO GOD ABOUT WHAT YOU SHOULD WEAR WHEN YOU GO TO THIS CHURCH" THE NEXT WEEK THE MAN WENT BACK TO THE CHURCH WITH THE SAME HOLES IN HIS PANTS AND SHIRT,THE PEOPLE DID NOT WANT TO TALK TO HIM AND AFTER THE SERVICE THE PREACHER CAME UP TO THE MAN AND ASKED "I THOUGHT YOU WAS GOING TO ASK GOD WHAT CLOTHES YOU SHOULD WEAR TO OUR CHURCH" THE MAN REPLIED "I DID" THEN THE PREACHER SAID "WELL,WHAT DID GOD SAY?" THE MAN REPLIED "GOD SAID HE DID NOT KNOW WHAT CLOTHES YOU SHOULD WEAR TO THAT CHURCH BECAUSE I NEVER BEEN THERE". THERE ARE A LOT OF SO CALLED CHURCHES THAT " GOD HAS NEVER BEEN THERE". WHAT PEOPLE ARE FEELING ARE COMING FROM THE GOD OF THIS WORLD, WHICH IS SATAN,THE DEVIL OR LUCIFER AND HE DOES HAVE A LOT OF DEMONS WHO LOVE TO MAKE YOU THINK ITS OK. RE-MEMBER INSIDE OF EVERY PERSON THERE IS A GOOD SPIRIT AND A EVIL SPIRIT YOU CAN NOT JUST PUSH IT AWAY. THESE TWO SPIRITS WILL BE WITH YOU FROM THE TIME YOU WERE BORN AND THE DAY YOU DIE. WHICH ONE IS THE STRONGEST MOST POWERFUL? WILL BE THE ONE YOU FEED THE MOST.YOU CAN JUMP UP AND DOWN AND ARGUE TILL THE COWS COME HOME AND TRY TO DRIVE OUT THIS EVIL SPIRIT BUT IT WILL NOT GO AWAY. ONCE YOU LEARN TO ACCEPT IT AND ONLY REMEMBER WHO EVER IS MORE POWER-FUL AND STRONGER IS THE ONE YOU FEED THE MOST. EVERYONE WANTS TO MAKE EVERYTHING COMPLI-CATED, THAT WAY THE FEW CAN BE IN CONTROL OF THE MAJORITY. ITS THE SAME WAY WITH PREACHERS,MOST MEAN WELL, BUT THEN GREED SITS IN AND THEY HAVE TO "PASS THE OFFERING PLATE AROUND" TO CONTROL YOU AND GET YOUR MONEY. DON'T GET ME WRONG ANY CHURCH MINISTRY, TO SURVIVE IT DOES TAKE A LOT OF MONEY, IF YOU WANT THIS FANCY CHURCH BUILDING, THEN SOMEONE HAS

TO PAY FOR IT IF YOU WANT PEOPLE TO PREACH,TEACH SING THEN MOST WNAT MONEY FOR THAT TO. RELI-GION IS A MULTI-MILLION DOLLAR INDUSTRY OR RACKET THAT GIVES YOU A FALSE SENSE OF SATISFAC-TION AND DEMANDS YOU COME BACK FOR MORE.IF THE REAL JESUS WAS ALIVE TODAY WOULD HE GO TO ANY OF THESE SO CALLED CHRISTIAN CHURCHES ON SUNDAY? WHEN THEY PASSED THE OFFERING PLATE AROUND WOULD THE REAL JESUS GIVE THEM ANY MONEY? WOULD THE REAL JESUS EAT PORK,CATFISH,SHRIMP OR LOBSTER? NO, DEEP DOWN IF YOU READ THE BIBLE AND UNDERSTAND THE LE-VITICAL LAW AND THE 10 COMMANDMENTS AND READ MATTHEW CHAPTER FIVE THEN YOU KNOW WHAT THE REAL JESUS(YAHSHUA) WOULD DO.REMEMBER THE PERSON WHO TOLD ADAM AND EVE IT WAS OK TO EAT THIS FORBIDDEN FRUIT BECAUSE YOU WILL NOT DIE, COULD THAT SAME PERSON BE TELLING PAUL AND OTHERS "ITS OK TO EAT WHATEVER YOU WANT TO THATS THE OLD LAW WE ARE SAVED BY GRACE AND NOT UNDER THE OLD LAW" REMEMBER YOU HAVE THESE TWO SPIRITS IN SIDE OF YOU, ONE OF GOOD AND ONE OF EVIL AND THEY ARE CONSTANTLY ARGUE-ING AND FIGHTING ALL THE TIME.YOU HAVE TO DECIDE FOR YOUR SELF WHAT IS RIGHT,I CAN NOT STAND BEFORE GOD FOR YOU, THAT IS SOMETHING YOU HAVE TO DO AND YOU WILL DO.IT DOES NOT MATTER WHAT CHURCH YOU GO TO OR WHAT RELI-GION YOU ARE,IT DOES NOT MATTER WHETHER YOU ARE A ATHEIST,EVOLUTIONIST OR JUST DON'T BELIEVE IN ANY HIGHER POWER CALLED GOD OR GODDESS BUT ASK YOUR SELF THIS, YOU HAVE TO HAVE A EARTH-LY FATHER AND A EARTHLY MOTHER TO CREATE YOU,MAYBE THE FATHER WAS ONLY THERE TO PLANT THE SEED AND IS GONE NOW BUT YOUR EARTHLY MOTHER TOOK THAT SEED AND NINE MONTHS LATER A CHILD WAS BORN, DID YOUR EARTHLY FATHER CREATE YOU? NO,HE ONLY PLANTED THE SEED, LOOK

AT ALL THE ANIMALS,FISH AND BIRDS 99% OF EVERY-THING WAS CREATED BY MALE AND FEMALE, SURE THERE ARE EXCEPTONS TO THIS RULE, THAT JUST SHOWS OUR CREATORS HAVE A SENSE OF HUMOR AND HAS GIVEN US THIS POWER TO CREATE LIFE. THE SAME WAY AND WE TAKE THIS GIFT AND ABUSE IT, WE MAKE IT INTO SOMETHING DIRTY OR XXX RATED. IF YOU ARE AT A CROSSROAD AND YOU HAVE TO DECIDE UPON USING YOUR GUT FEELING AND COMMON SENSE AND ASK QUESTIONS,THINK ABOUT WHAT IS REALLY RIGHT. REMEMBER THE ONLY STUPID QUESTION IS THE ONE YOU NEVER ASK. NO ONE IS PERFECT, WE ALL MAKE MISTAKES,IF I AM WRONG, SHOW ME BUT "ON THE OTHER HAND" IF I AM RIGHT, THEN JOIN ME. I NEED A LOT OF PEOPLE TO MAKE THIS MINISTRY TO WORK. OUR CHURCH IS CALLED BROKEN WING MINISTRY BE-CAUSE OUR WINGS HAVE BEEN BROKEN BECAUSE OF OUR SIN. WE ARE NOT SOME CULT OR NEW AGE RELI-GION.YES SOME OF US ARE VAMPYRES, BUT MOST WILL KEEP THE LAW AND DENY IT. IN TIME, PEOPLE WILL READ THIS BOOK AND THEY WILL COME OUT OF THE CLOSET. SOME PEOPLE SUPPRESS THEIR PAST LIFES AND TRY TO FOLLOW "MODERN RELIGION" TO GO WITH THE FLOW AND NOT CAUSE ANY PROBLEMS. THATS OK WITH ME. I KNOW WHO I AM. DO YOU KNOW WHO YOU ARE? HAVE YOU EVER DREAMED YOU LIVED A PAST LIFE? HAVE YOU EVER BEEN TO A PLACE YOU NEVER BEEN DURING THIS LIFETIME BUT DEEP DOWN FEELS FAMILIAR? OUR RELIGION GOES BACK TO WHAT ADAM AND EVE WOULD GO TO,DID ADAM ONLY LIVE ONE LIFE? NO HE HAS LIVED MANY LIFES.IS HIS SPIRIT SOUL STILL AROUND TODAY? YES, OF COURSE. WHAT ABOUT ABEL? WE KNOW THAT CAIN KILLED HIM WHAT HAPPENED TO HIS SPIRIT SOUL? IS IT JUST LAYING IN THE GROUND WAITING FOR THIS FUTURE RAPTURE? WHAT ABOUT NOAH AND HIS FAMILY? ARE THEY JUST DEAD AND THAT IS IT? ARE THEY SETTING AROUND IN HEAVEN PLAYING ON A HARP? WHAT ABOUT ABRAHAM

AND HIS FAMILY? MOST OF ALL WHAT ABOUT THE REAL JESUS(YAHSHUA) CHRIST? DO YOU KNOW THAT THE NAME JESUS IS ONLY CAME ABOUT IN THE FIFTEENTH CENTURY? BEFORE THAT THE ORIGINAL HEBREW LANGUAGE NEVER HAD THE LETTER J HIS REAL HEBREW NAME IS YAHSHUA,BUT FOR THE LAST FIVE HUNDRED YEARS THE ENGLISH KINGS WHO HELP CREATE THIS PRINTING PRESS AND CREATED WHAT THEY CALL THE "KING JAMES VERSION" ADDED THE SHAKESPEARE TYPE LANGUAGE. CHANGING THE YAHSHUA TO A ENGLISH VERSION OF JESUS AND THE HEBREW YAHWEH WAS CHANGED TO THE ENGLISH VERSION OF JEHOVAH AND THE GODDESS,SHEKINAH WAS HIDDEN BECAUSE THEY DID NOT WANT WOMAN TO HAVE ANY POWER, SO THEY CALLED HER THE HOLY GHOST,HOLY SPIRIT OR COMFORTER.THEN TO ADD INSULT THEY CALLED THEM A MALE ALSO. SO THEY HELPED CREATE THIS SO CALLED TRINITY OF A MALE GOD, A MALE SON OF GOD AND A MALE HOLY SPIRIT, AND BURNED ANYONE WHO DID NOT BELIEVE ACCORDING TO THEIR BELIEF. I WAS ONE OF THOSE WHO WAS BURNED,I HAVE HAD THIS RE-OCCURING DREAM AGAIN AND AGAIN. THEM TELLING ME TO REPENT AND ACCEPT JEHOVAH,AND WORSHIP HIM ON SUNDAY OR BURN IN HELL FOREVER AND EVER. I WAS READY TO GET OUT OF THIS LIFE AND I KNEW I NEEDED TO EXPERIENCE THIS PAIN AND AGONY,THE MELTING FLESH, THE PAIN,A HORRIBLE WAY TO DIE,BUT NOT AS BAD AS THE WAY MY YAHSHUAH HAD TO DIE, SO I CALLED UPIN MY YAHWEH AND MY SHEKINAH TO HELP ME BARE THIS PAIN AND I FELT THE COMFORT AND ACCEPTED MY PUNISHMENT.ALL OF THIS BECAUSE SOME PEOPLE,I THOUGHT WERE MY FRIENDS BETRAYED ME TO GAIN POWER. THE WORLD WAS FULL OF GREED,BACK STABBING AND POWER HUNGRY PEOPLE. IT HAS NOT CHANGED, THE WORLD IS STILL DOING THE SAME THING. WE JUST DO NOT PERSECUTE YOU IN THE SAME WAY. WE SIMPLY TRUMP UP CHARGES AND COMMIT

YOU TO A JAIL OR MENTAL INSTITUTION. YOU DON'T BELIEVE ME? LOOK AROUND. "YOU HAVE EYES BUT YOU DO NOT SEE, YOU HAVE EARS BUT YOU DO NOT HEAR." OVER HALF THE PEOPLE IN MENTAL INSTITUTION'S ARE NOT CRAZY, JUST ON DIFFERENT LEVELS OR STEPS. SOME OF THEIR PAST LIFE WAS REMEMBERED AND THEY HAVE A HARD TIME ACCEPTING IT. A STORY IN ONE OF MY OTHER BOOKS WAS ABOUT A MAN IN A MENTAL HOSPITAL. THE NURSE'S ASKED HIM WHAT HE WANTED FOR HIS BIRTHDAY AND HE SAID A WHEEL BARREL. THE NURSE ASKED WHY? HE TOLD HER, EVERY PERSON IN HERE HAS A LOT OF PROBLEMS, I COULD TAKE ALL THESE PROBLEMS AND TAKE THEM AWAY IN THE WHEEL BARREL. SO THEY ALL GOT TOGETHER AND BOUGHT HIM A WHEEL BARREL. EVERYTHING WAS FINE FOR AWHILE THEN ONE DAY THE NURSE SAW HIM DRAGGING THE WHEEL BARREL AROUND UP SIDE DOWN. SHE ASKED WHAT HAPPENED? HE TOLD HER THE WHEEL BARREL GOT SO HEAVY FROM TAKING IN EVERYONE'S PROBLEMS THAT HE COULD NOT PUSH IT. SHE THOUGHT FOR A MOMENT AND SAID WHAT IF YOU GET THIS INVISIBLE SHOVEL AND DIG A INVISIBLE HOLE, THEN YOU CAN BURY ALL THESE TROUBLES IN IT? HE THOUGHT FOR A MOMENT THEN AGREED. SOMETIMES WE NEED TO TAKE ALL OUR PROBLEMS AND GET THIS INVISIBLE SHOVEL AND DIG THIS INVIS-IBLE HOLE AND BURY ALL OUR PROBLEMS IN IT. WILL THEY GO AWAY? ONLY IF YOU DIG THE HOLE DEEP ENOUGH, THEN FORGET WHERE YOU BURIED THEM AT SO YOU CAN NOT GO BACK AND DIG THEM UP LATER.

CHAPTER 4

THIS WILL BE CHAPTER NUMBER FOUR THE FEMALE SIDE OF GOD OR THE GODDESS.THRU OUT HISTORY MANY CIVILIZATIONS HAVE CALLED OUR GODDESS BY MANY NAMES. I STILL,TO THIS DAY FEEL MORE COMFORTABLE WITH SHEKINAH. AS A VAMPIRE,LIVING MANY LIFETIMES, I RECALL MOST OF WHAT HAPPENED DURING MY PREVIOUS LIFE. SOMETIMES I CHOOSE TO ERASE FROM MY MIND SOME OF THE DULL,BAD PARTS. IT WOULD BE EASY TO SAY I WAS SOME IMPORTANT KING OR NAPOLEAN OR PRESIDENT.MOST OF THE TIME ESPECIALLY DURING THE LAST FIVE CENTURIES I DID MY PART AS FAR AS FIGHTING A WAR IF CALLED UPON. TRIED TO OBEY WHAT EVER POWER, WEATHER IT WAS A KING,QUEEN OR PRESIDENT.I HAD MY LITTLE GROUP OF FOLLOWERS AND REALIZED IT WAS EASY FOR ME TO USE MY POWERS AS A PREACHER. SO I WENT

TO SEMINARY AND TOOK ALL THE THEOLOGY CLASSES I COULD AND BECAME ORDAINED IN WHAT EVER RELIGION WAS THE MOST POWERFUL AT THE TIME. THIS HAD TO MAKE ME SUPPRESS MY REAL BELIEFS AND FOLLOW A BUNCH OF SUNDAY WORSHIPPING,EATING ANYTHING BUNCH OF PHARASEE AND HYPOCRITES BUT I WOULD TELL THEM WHAT THEY WANTED TO HEAR,PASSED THE OFFERING PLATE AROUND AND NOT ONLY TOOK THEIR MONEY BUT ALSO TOOK THEIR POWER. WOMAN LOVED ME AND I NOT ONLY GAVE THEM THE ORGASM THEY YEARNED FOR BUT ALSO TOOK THEIR POWER AND ENERGY. I FEED ON IT,WOKE UP IN THE MORNING HUNGRY,DEBATING ON WHO I WOULD RAVAGE THIS TIME. I WAS HUNG FROM A TREE BY A JEALOUS HUSBAND WHO JUST HAPPENED TO BE MARRIED TO THE MOST BEAUTIFUL RED HEAD IN TOWN. I KNEW HE WAS THE SHERIFF BUT THAT ONLY MADE IT MORE EXCITING.RIGHT BEFORE I DIED SHE CAME TO ME AND TOLD ME SHE WAS PREGNANT WITH MY CHILD BUT SHE WOULD MAKE HIM BELIEVE IT WAS HIS. I CAME BACK IN MY NEXT LIFE AS A RED HEADED GIRL,MY LOVERS DAUGHTER , HE THOUGHT I WAS HIS CHILD, AND HE DIED BY A GUN MAN WHO WAS FASTER ON THE DRAW, WHEN I WAS TWO YEARS OLD. NOW THE WOMAN WHO WAS MY SECRET LOVER IN ONE LIFE,BECAME MY MOTHER.I WAS HER ONLY DAUGHTER AND I TOLD HER ABOUT ALL THE LIFES I HAD LIVED AND HOPED TO SEE HER AGAIN IN A FUTURE LIFE. I TOOK CARE OF HER IN HER OLD AGE AND SHE DIED PEACEFULLY AT THE OLD AGE OF 74. I HAVE ALREADY HINTED AROUND IN MY PREVIOUS CHAPTERS ABOUT THE FEMALE SIDE OF GOD OR WHAT IN THE BIBLE TALKS ABOUT AS THE HOLY GHOST,HOLY SPIRIT OR COMFORTER. REMEMBER THE MAJORITY OF THE PEOPLE INVOLVED IN CREATING THE BIBLE WERE MEN AND THRU OUT HISTORY, MEN REALIZED THAT WOMAN HAVE A LOT OF POWER, SO TO SUPPRESS THIS POWER THEY TRY TO TAKE IT AWAY. THRU-OUT HISTO-

RY A LOT OF CIVILIZATIONS TRIED TO DO THE THREE STEPS TO HARMONY AND THAT IS, FIRST YOU HAVE TO HAVE EQUALITY,IF YOU HAVE EQUALITY THEN SECOND YOU CAN ACHIEVE BALANCE AND IF YOU CAN ACHIEVE BALANCE THEN YOUR SOCIETY OR CIVILIZATION WILL HAVE HARMONY. I WROTE A BOOK TITLED "HARMONY, THE GREATEST STORY NEVER TOLD " BY PASTOR MELVIN ABERCROMBIE UNDER TRAFFORD PUBLISH-ING. THERE IS 14 CHAPTERS AND EACH ASK A LOT OF QUESTIONS AND ANSWERS,OBVIOUSLY THE DEMONIC,EVIL POWERS THAT RULE OVER THIS WORLD DOES NOT WANT YOU OR ANYONE ELSE TO READ THIS BECAUSE THEN YOU MAY UNDERSTAND THE SIMPLE TRUTH. MY OTHER BOOK WAS WRITTEN ABOUT SOME OF THE QUESTIONS CHILDREN ASK IT TO HAS 14 CHAP-TERS WITH EACH CHAPTER ASKING A QUESTION AND BETWEEN EACH CHAPTER I PLACED ONE OF MY POEMS AS A FREE GIFT. MOST PEOPLE ARE MAD BECAUSE I WOULD TITLE A BOOK ASKING THIS SIMPLE QUESTION BUT EVERYONE NEEDS TO KNOW THE ANSWER IT IS ALSO LISTED UNDER TRAFFORD PUBLISHING AND IS TITLED "DOES GOD HAVE A PENIS?" THIS IS A QUESION A CHILD WOULD ASK BECAUSE MOST CHURCHES AND RELIGION WANT TO THINK OF OUR CREATOR AS SOME FORMLESS, GENDERLESS BALL OF FIRE OR ENERGY.IF YOU READ GENESIS CHAPTER SIX THEN YOU REALIZE THE ANGELS MUST HAVE SOME KIND OF A MALE RE-PRODUCTIVE ORGANS OR HOW ELSE COULD THEY HAVE SEX WITH THE "DAUGHTERS OF MEN" IF GOD DID WHAT THE LAWS OF THE UNITED STATES AND THE CHRISTIANS SAY HE DID, THEN GOD WOULD GO TO JAIL FOR STATUATORY RAPE,BE LABELED A SEX OFFENDER,HAVE A FELONY RECORD AND BE LABELED AS HAVING SEX WITH A MINOR BECAUSE EVERYONE KNOWS THAT THE VIRGIN MARY WAS UNDER THE AGE OF 18. EVEN IF THIS WAS A CONSENTING SEXUAL AFFAIR DID GOD MARRY THE VIRGIN MARY? WHAT DO YOU CALL A CHILD BORN OUT OF WEDLOCK? A BASTARD

CHILD. DO YOU THINK OF JESUS AS A "BASTARD CHILD?" SOME RELIGIONS DO LIKE THE ISLAM,AND JEWISH PEOPLE THEY CALL CHRISTIANS "INFIDELS AND SHOULD ALL BE DESTROYED" HOW COULD GOD DO THIS SUCH A THING? EVEN UNDER THE HEBREW/ JEWISH LAW STOP RIGHT NOW AND READ DEUTERON-OMY CHAPTER 22 ESPECIALLY VERSES 23 ON. SO AC-CORDING TO GODS OWN LAW IF GOD DID WHAT THE CHRISTIANS SAY HE DID THEN ACCORDING TO THIS BIBLE THEN GOD AND THE VIRGIN MARY BOTH SHOULD BE STONED TO DEATH HIM FOR HAVING SEX TO A VIRGIN WHO WAS PROMISED TO ANOTHER MAN (JOSEPH) AND MARY FOR NOT CRYING OUT. SO THE QUESTION YOU HAVE TO ASK IS WHY DID GOD DO THIS? WHY DID GOD FIND A VIRGIN THAT WAS AL-READY PROMISED TO SOME ONE ELSE? COULD GOD NOT FIND A VIRGIN THAT WAS NOT BETROTHED OR PROMISED TO SOMEONE? IF GOD CREATED ADAM AND EVE BY SNAPPING HIS FINGERS OR SPEAK AND THEY WERE THEIR THEN WHY DIDN'T GOD CREATE JESUS,THE SON OF GOD THE SAME WAY? WOULD GOD BREAK HIS OWN LAWS THAT HE GAVE TO MOSES? RE-MEMBER THE UNITED STATES WAS NOT CREATED THEN. JUST LIKE WE HAVE 12 YEARS OF SCHOOLING FOR OUR CHILDREN, WE WAIT UNTIL A CHILD IS FIVE OR SIX BEFORE ENROLLING THEM IN SCHOOL BUT BACK THEN THE HEBREW/JEWISH TYPE PEOPLE START-ED THEIR TRAINING AT BIRTH AND 12 YEARS LATER THEY HAVE ACHIEVED THE SAME RESULTS. ON A CHILDS 13TH BIRTHDAY A BOY WILL GO THRU HIS "BAR MITSVAH" AND BECOME A MAN READY TO GO TO WORK,USUALLY IN HIS FATHERS BUSINESS.THE SAME AS WITH A GIRL,USUALLY WHEN A GIRL STARTS HER PERIOD OR THE "ISSUE OF BLOOD" THEN A GIRL WILL GO THRU WHAT IS CALLED A "BAT MITSVAH " WHICH IS THE SAME THEY ARE CONSIDERED AS A ADULT AND ABLE TO BE MARRIED THRU USUALLY A ARRANGED MARRIAGE. SO ACCORDING TO HEBREW/JEWISH LAW

SHE IS CONSIDERED AS A ADULT.IF BOTH PARTIES ARE CONSENTING THEN NO LAW IS BROKEN SO THE LAWS OF THE UNITED STATES WOULD NOT APPLY. BUT THEN YOU ASK WHAT ABOUT THE LEVITICAL/DEUTERONO-MY LAW? WAS THE VIRGIN MARY PROMISED/BE-TROTHED TO JOSEPH? YES IF YOU READ THE BIBLE YOU WILL SEE THAT JOSEPH FOUND OUT THAT SHE WAS PREGNANT AND HE KNEW HE DID NOT HAVE SEX WITH HER. HE KNEW HE HAD THE POWER TO GO TO THE RABBI AND DEMAND HER DEATH BY STONING AND HE WOULD HAVE THE RIGHT TO THROW THE FIRST STONE. THEN HE ALSO KNEW THAT SOME MAN HAS TAKEN AWAY HER VIRGINITY AND HE WOULD HAVE A RIGHT TO FIND THIS MAN AND DO THE SAME THING AC-CORDING TO HEBREW/JEWISH LAW. SO WAS GOD GUILTY OF BREAKING HIS OWN LAWS? SHOULD GOD BE STONED TO DEATH ACCORDING TO HIS OWN LAWS. WOULD JOSEPH THROW THE FIRST STONE KNOWING HE HAD THE RIGHT TO. REMEMBER NO ONE ELSE CAN THROW A STONE UNTIL THE PERSON MAKING THE AC-CUSATION THROWS THE FIRST STONE.THE LAW STATES THEY WILL BE GIVEN A FAIR TRIAL,IF FOUND GUILTY THEN PLACED IN A PIT AND THE PERSON MAKING THE ACCUSATION IS ALLOWED TO THROW THE FIRST STONE. IF HE DOES NOT THROW A STONE THEN NO ONE ELSE CAN AND THE PEOPLE WILL BE BANISHED FROM THEIR SOCIETY.SOME SAY IF HE DOES NOT CAST A STONE THEN OTHER FAMILY MEMBERS CAN PROTEST AND DEMAND RESULTS THEN THE RABBI HAS TO DECIDE. THE FINAL RESULTS WILL BE UP TO THE LEADERS,THE ELDERS AND RABBI. SO NOW IF YOU IMAGINE THAT IN THE BEGINNING THERE WAS A MALE GOD AND A FEMALE GODDESS AND ADAM WAS CRE-ATED IN THE IMAGE OF THIS MALE GOD INCLUDING ALL THE REPRODUCTIVE ORGANS TO CREATE LIFE AND THAT EVE WAS CREATED IN THE IMAGE OF OUR MOTHER GODDESS INCLUDING ALL FEMALE REPRO-DUCTIVE ORGANS TO CREATE LIFE. NOW GENESIS

MAKES SENSE BECAUSE IT SAYS THAT ADAM AND EVE
WERE CREATED IN THE IMAGE OF US IN OUR IMAGE
THIS IS NOT SINGULAR BUT PLURAL. SO NOW WE UN-
DERSTAND WHY SO MANY CIVILIZATIONS HAVE THIS
MALE GOD AND FEMALE GODDESS LIKE THE EGYP-
TIANS WHO WORSHIPPED OSIRIS AND ISIS THEN
DURING JESUS LIFETIME THE POWERS IN CHARGE
WERE THE ROMANS WHO HAD AS A MALE GOD, JUPITER
AND AS THE GODDESS JUNO. THEN THE GREEKS HAD
ZEUS AS A MALE GOD AND HERA AS THE GODDESS, THEN
MOST ALL OF EUROPE WAS DIVIDED INTO TWO MAIN
FACTIONS CALLED CELTIC AND TEUTONIC THE CELT-
ICS HAD CERRUNOS AS THE MALE GOD AND CERRID-
WEN AS THE FEMALE GODDESS AND THE TEUTONICS
HAD ODIN AS THEIR MALE GOD AND FREYA AS THE
FEMALE GODDESS. WE COULD GO ON ABOUT A LOT OF
OTHER CIVILIZATIONS, THE MAYAN, NATIVE INDIANS
AND DIFFERENT COUNTRIES WE COULD WRITE A
BOOK ABOUT ALL THE DIFFERENT NAMES AND THERE
ARE BOOKS WRITTEN THAT TEACH US AND SOME CALL
IT MYTHOLOGY AND ALL PART OF OUR WILD IMAGI-
NATION. IF YOU FORGET EVERYTHING ELSE AND ONLY
THINK ABOUT COMMON SENSE THEN ITS NOT ALL
THAT COMPLICATED IF YOU THINK ABOUT WHERE
EVER THERE IS MENTION IN THE BIBLE ABOUT A HOLY
SPIRIT, A HOLY GHOST OR COMFORTER AND INSTEAD
OF BEING ANOTHER MALE BUT A FEMALE THEN YOU
WILL HAVE THE TRUE TRINITY A MALE GOD A FEMALE
GODDESS AND A MALE "SON OF GOD" NOW THE BIBLE
MAKES SENSE SO IF YOU GO INTO LUKES VERSION OF
WHAT HAPPENED IN THE BIBLE THEN YOU WILL SEE
THAT THE HOLY GHOST WENT INTO THE VIRGIN MARY
FIRST. IF THIS WAS A MALE SPIRIT THEN WHY WOULD A
MALE HOLY GHOST GO INTO THE VIRGIN MARY FIRST?
DOES THIS MAKE SENSE TO YOU? IF THE HOLY GHOST
WAS THE FEMALE GODDESS SIDE OF GOD AND SHE
WENT INTO THE VIRGIN MARY FIRST THEN WHEN
GOD, THE MALE HAD SEX WITH THE VIRGIN MARY HE

WAS ACTUALLY HAVING SEX WITH HIS WIFE WHICH IS LEGAL AND KOSHER THEY USED THE VIRGIN MARY AS A VESSEL TO MERELY BRING FORTH A CHILD. THE CATHOLICS HAVE A SAYING CALLED "IMMACULATE CONCEPTION" WHICH MEANS AFTER THE CHILD JESUS WAS BORN THEN THE VIRGIN MARY WAS TESTED AND FOUND TO STILL BE A VIRGIN SO JOSEPH,BY HONORING WHAT GOD ASKED HIM TO, RECIEVED A VIRGIN BRIDE AFTER ALL.SOME OTHER CHURCHES RECOGNIZE THIS "IMMACUALTE CONCEPTION" AND WE, AS MEMBERS OF BROKEN WING MINISTRY ACCEPT THIS AS PART OF OUR DOCTRINE AND TEACHING. SO THE BOTTOM LINE THEN DID GOD BREAK ANY LAWS? IF HE DID THIS TODAY IN THE UNITED STATES HE WOULD BREAK OUR LAWS BUT THE UNITED STATES WAS NOT CREATED. DID HE BREAK ANY HEBREW/JEWISH LAW? SOME PEOPLE STILL WHO ARE ORTHODOX, SAY YES AND DO NOT ACCEPT THIS. TO THEM GOD SHOULD HAVE USED A VIRGIN NOT PROMISED OR BETROTHED TO SOMEONE ELSE. WE WILL NEVER KNOW THE ANSWER OF WHY OUR FATHER GOD AND MOTHER GODDESS DID IT THIS WAY. HOW WAS ANGELS CREATED? DID OUR MALE GOD AND FEMALE GODDESS CREATE THEM FIRST? DID THEY HAVE WINGS? WE DO KNOW THAT A THIRD OF THE ANGELS WERE CAST OUT OF HEAVEN,WHERE DID THEY GO? COULD OUR GOD AND GODDESS CREATE THIS WORLD TO GIVE THE FALLEN ANGELS SOMETHING TO RULE OVER? WHY WHERE THEY CAST OUT OF HEAVEN? COULD THE FIRST BORN MAYBE BE CALLED LUCIFER AND EVENTUALLY WANT AND EXPECT TO BE A RULER SOMEDAY? IF GOD NEVER DIES THEN WHAT DOES THE FIRST BORN RULE OVER? COULD THIS BE WHY THEY HAD A REBELLION IN THE FIRST PLACE? BY CREATING THIS EARTH TO GIVE THE FALLEN ANGELS SOMETHING TO RULE OVER THEN WATCH AS THEY CREATED ALL THIS EVIL AND GOD SAW ALL THE EVIL AND DESTROYED IT BY THE FLOOD?WHAT HAPPENED AFTER THE FLOOD? DID ALL

THESE PEOPLE JUST DIE? DID ANYBODY CROSS OVER? WE KNOW THAT NOAH HAD THREE SONS BUT HE ALSO HAD MANY DAUGHTERS. THE THREE SONS HAD WIVES SO DID ANY OF THEM GET PREGNANT DURING THIS TIME? COULD SOME VAMPIRES GO INTO THE NEXT LIFE AS A CHILD OF NOAH? OR SHEM,HAM OR JAPETH? YAHWEH TOLD THEM TO BE FRUITFUL AND MULTIPLY. I REMEMBER THE FLOOD,ONE OF MY POEMS TALKS ABOUT THIS. I WAS NOBODY SPECIAL LIKE NOAH BUT ONLY A CHILD. BACK THEN A GIRL WAS NOT GIVEN MUSH POWER SO THEY DID NOT MENTION THEM IN THE BIBLE TO MUCH. EVERYONE WANTS TO BLAME EVE BECAUSE OF ALL OF OUR SINS. DID EVE POINT A GUN TO ADAMS HEAD AND MAKE HIM EAT? NO ITS EASY TO BLAME A WOMAN AND THEN FOR THOUSANDS OF YEARS SUPPRESS ALL THEIR RIGHTS TO JUSTIFY YOURSELF. DID GOD KNOW THAT ADAM AND EVE WOULD EAT THIS FORBIDDEN FRUIT? ACCORDING TO THE BIBLE HE WALKED THRU THE GARDEN AND WANTED TO KNOW WHY THEY WERE HIDING? I THOUGHT GOD KNEW EVERYTHING? IF HE KNOWS THE HAIRS ON YOUR HEAD, THEN HE SHOULD KNOW THAT EVENTUALLY THEY WOULD BE TEMPTED, BUT KNOWING THESE THINGS WHY DID HE KICK THEM OUT OF THE GARDEN OF EDEN? WHERE WAS JESUS(YAHSHUA) DURING ALL THIS? IF YOU READ JOHN CHAPTER ONE IT SAYS JESUS(YAHSHUA) WAS THE WORD AND THE WORD WAS WITH HIM FROM THE BEGIN-NING? SOME PREACHERS SAY GOD AND JESUS WERE THEIR IN THE BEGINNING AND THEY WERE ALL ONE PERSON. THIS IS THE BIGGEST LIE CHRISTIANITY HAS EVER TOLD YOU. IN THE FIRST PLACE IF GOD AND YAH-SHUA WERE ONE,THEN WHY ARE THEY CALLED BY DIF-FERENT NAMES? IF THEY ARE ONE THEN WHO IS ON THE RIGHT HAND SIDE OF GOD? IF THEY ARE ONE THEN WHO IS YAHSHUA CALLING OUT RIGHT BEFORE HE DIES? IF THEY ARE ONE THEN WHEN JOHN THE BAPTIST, BAPTIZED YAHSHUA WHAT HAPPENED? A

VOICE FROM HEAVEN SAY THIS IS "MY SON WHO I AM PLEASED"? HOW CAN THEY BE ONE? WHEN EVEN THE DEVIL WAS SENT TO TEMPT YAHSHUA WHAT HAPPENED? CAN SATAN TAKE GOD THE FATHER UP ON A MOUNTAIN TOP? CAN SATAN TALK TO HIS FATHER AND SAY JUMP OFF THIS MOUNTAIN AND SOME ANGELS WILL CATCH YOU? DOES SATAN HAVE THE POWER TO TELL HIS FATHER TO BOW DOWN AND WORSHIP HIM AND HE WOULD GIVE ALL THIS TO HIM? DOES GOD OWN ALL THIS OR DOES SATAN? EVEN SATAN SAID " THIS SURELY IS THE SON OF GOD AND WHEN THE DISCIPLES ASKED YAHSHUA WHAT IS THE PROPER WAY TO PRAY AND WE HAVE WHAT IS CALLED THE "LORDS PRAYER" YAHSHUA DID NOT SAY TO PRAY TO ME BECAUSE I AM GOD, NO YAHSHUA SAID "WE PRAY TO"OUR FATHER WHO IS IN HEAVEN,BLESSED BE HIS NAME, HIS KINGDOM COME, HIS WILL BE DONE,ON EARTH AS IT IS IN HEAVEN.I HAVE LIVED MANY LIFETIMES. EACH TIME I DIE MY SPIRIT /SOUL DOES GO TO HEAVEN. "EVERY KNEE SHALL BOW, EVERY TONGUE SHALL CONFESS" I STAND BEFORE THE REAL TRINITY, MY FATHER GOD, YAHWEH, MY MOTHER GODDESS,SHEKINAH ON HIS LEFT SIDE AND MY YAHSHUA,MY BIG BROTHER, ON HIS RIGHT SIDE INTERCEDDING ON MY BEHALF. I AM ACCOUNTABLE AND I AM RESPONSIBLE FOR WHAT EVER I DID DURING THIS LIFETIME. YAHSHUA DID NOT DIE ON THE CROSS FORR MY SINS, I AM NOT SAVED BY GRACE. YAHSHUA DIED ON THE CROSS TO DO AWAY WITH THE OLD SACRIFICIAL LAW. WHEN WE COMMIT A SIN WE CAN NOT GO FIND A CALF,LAMB OR OTHER ANIMAL AND TAKE IT TO THE HIGH PRIEST OR RABBI TO DIE FOR US. THAT ANIMAL DID NOTHING WRONG,WHY SHOULD IT DIE FOR SOMETHING YOU DID? ALL THESE FALSE CHURCH'S TELLING YOU DON'T WORRY,GIVE ME YOUR MONEY AND I WILL PUT IN A GOOD WORD FOR YOU,DON'T WORRY YOU ARE SAVED BY "GRACE" IS ALL WRONG. THIS 40,60,80 YEARS YOU ARE LIVING NOW AND YOU HOPE, WHEN YOU DO FI-

NALLY DIE SOMEONE WILL PUT A GOOD WORD FOR YOU AND YOU GET TO GO TO HEAVEN IS A BUNCH OF BULL. DEEP DOWN YOU KNOW YOU HAVE LIVED IN A PAST LIFE. MOST DO NOT WANT TO REMEMBER. WHAT ABOUT ALL THESE CRAZY DREAMS YOU HAVE? DO DREAMS MEAN ANYTHING? WHEN YAHSHUA TRIED TO PREACH TO PEOPLE, MOST DID NOT UNDERSTAND BE-CAUSE HE SPOKE IN PARABLES. ONLY THOSE WHO WERE READY TO UNDERSTAND WOULD UNDERSTAND, ITS THE SAME WITH THIS BOOK. SOME WHO READ THIS BOOK WILL NOT UNDERSTAND ,BUT THEN LATER IT WILL HIT YOU AND YOUR EYES WILL BE OPEN. MY PRAYER IS FOR," NOT MY WILL BUT YAHWEH'S WILL BE DONE." IF YAHWEH WANTS THIS BOOK TO BE WRITTEN THEN IT WILL HAPPEN. IF YAHWEH WANTS MILLIONS OF PEOPLE TO READ THIS BOOK THEN THE MONEY WILL BE USED TO HELP OUR BROKEN WING MINISTRY. SHALOM

CHAPTER 5

THIS WILL BE THE FIFTH CHAPTER, RE-INCARNATION.I REPEAT I BELIEVE IN RE-INCARNATION. I NOT ONLY BELIEVE BUT I KNOW I HAVE LIVED MANY LIVES. I AM TEMPORARY STUCK IN THIS PHYSICAL BODY. I KNOW THAT I AM A VAMPIRE. I ABSORB YOUR ENERGY. I DO NOT DRINK BLOOD,I AM NOT AFRAID OF THE LIGHT,ACTUALLY THE LIGHT COMES FROM THE SUN WHICH IS RULED OVER BY LUCIFER,THE FIRST BORN SON OF GOD AND THE GODDESS. YOU SAY HE IS EVIL? WHAT IS EVIL? HOW DO YOU KNOW WHAT IS EVIL UNLESS SOMEONE TEACHES YOU?WHO WOULD BE A BETTER TEACHER? WHEN I FIRST STARTED DOING THE ROUGH DRAFT OF THIS BOOK, I KNEW THERE WAS FIVE MAIN TOPICS I WANTED TO GET ACROSS,(1) THE FEMALE SIDE OF GOD (2) THE SABBATH OR 7TH DAY OF REST.(3) THE KOSHER FOOD OR CLEAN/UNCLEAN FOODS WE SHOULD EAT. (4)RE-IN-

CARNATION AND (5)THE ONE TRUE CHURCH,THE ONE TRUE RELIGION. DID JESUS TEACH RE-INCARNATION? YES WE BELIEVE MOST HEBREW/JEWISH PEOPLE UNDERSTAND THE BASIC FUNDALMENTAL IDEA BEHIND RE-INCARNATION. THE DISCIPLES WERE CONSTANTLY BEING ASKED QUESTIONS BY JESUS TO FIND OUT WHAT THEY KNEW. ONE EXAMPLE WAS MATTHEW CHAPTER 16 VERSES 13-20, MARK CHAPTER 8 VERSES 27-30 AND LUKE CHAPTER 9 VERSES 18-21. WHAT WE FIND IN ALL THREE IS JESUS ASKING THE DISCIPLES WHO DO THE PEOPLE SAY THAT I AM? THEIR ANSWER IS SOME SAY YOU ARE ELIAS,SOME SAY YOU ARE JOHN THE BAPTIST COMING BACK OR SOME OTHER PROPHET THAT HAS DIED AND ARE COMING BACK IN YOUR NEXT LIFE. EVEN THRU OUT THE BIBLE IT IS MENTIONED THAT JESUS WAS HERE FROM THE BEGINNING ALONG WITH THE FATHER. IN JOHN CHAPTER 9 VERSES 1-5 THE DISCIPLES ARE TALKING ABOUT A MAN WHO WAS BORN BLIND,HOW COULD THIS PERSON BEING BORN BLIND COMMIT ANY SIN DURING THIS LIFE? DID HE COMMIT A SIN IN HIS PAST LIFE OR WAS THIS THE SINS OF THE FATHER/MOTHER BEING PASSED DOWN?.THE DISCIPLES NOT ONLY KNEW ABOUT RE-INCARNATION BUT UNDERSTOOD THAT A SIN CAN BE CARRIED OVER FROM ONE LIFE TO THE NEXT. ONE REASON THE HEBREW/JEWISH PEOPLE DID NOT LIKE JESUS WAS BECAUSE HE WAS GOING AROUND HEALING PEOPLE OF THEIR SINS. THEY KNEW THE PEOPLE HAD THESE DISEASE'S,BLIND,AND DEAF BECAUSE OF PAST LIFE SINS AND THEY DID NOT LIKE JESUS HEALING THEM.THEIR LOGIC WAS,IF JESUS HEALED THAT PERSON THEN THEY MIGHT FEEL LIKE THEY CAN COMMIT THE SIN AGAIN,DON'T WORRY, WHAT EVER SIN I COMMIT ALL I HAVE TO DO IS GO TO JESUS AND HE WILL HEAL ME. THERE IS NO MORE ACCOUNTABILITY OR RESPONSIBILITY.JUST LIKE THE FALSE CHURCHES OF TODAY, GO AHEAD AND COMMIT WHAT EVER SIN YOU WANT TO JUST GO TO ANY TYPICAL CHURCH,PUT SOME MONEY IN THEIR OFFERING PLATE AND ASK GOD

TO FORGIVE YOU AND YOU GET TO GO TO HEAVEN WHEN YOU DIE. YOU DON'T EVEN HAVE TO BUY A CALF OR SHEEP NO MORE BECAUSE WE ARE NO LONGER UNDER THE SACRIFICIAL LAW. DID JESUS DIE ON THE CROSS FOR YOUR SINS? NO JESUS DID DIE ON THE CROSS TO DO AWAY WITH THE OLD SACRIFICIAL LAW. HE WAS THE ULTIMATE SACRIFICE AND WE ARE NO LONGER UNDER THAT PART OF THE LAW. THAT IS THE ONLY LAW THAT HAS BEEN CHANGED.ARE WE STILL UNDER THE LAW? OF COURSE NOTHING HAS CHANGED EXCEPT THE DOING AWAY OF THE SACRIFICIAL LAW. READ MATTHEW CHAPTER FIVE VERSES 17-19. WHAT IS JESUS TELLING US? "THAT HE DID NOT COME HERE TO CHANGE THE LAW NOT ONE DOTING OF A I OR CROSSING OF A T BUT ANYONE SHALL BREAK ONE OF THESE COMMAND-MENTS AND SHALL TEACH MEN SO SHALL BE CALLED LEAST IN THE KINGDOM OF HEAVEN" SO THAT MEANS ABOUT 99% OF ALL SO CALLED CHRISTIAN CHURCHES TODAY ARE BREAKING THIS DIRECT COMMANDMENT FROM JESUS. THEN WE WONDER WHY WE ARE HAVING ALL THE PROBLEMS AND WE ARE "SCATTERED AND CONFUSED". IN MY PREVIOUS LESSONS I MENTIONED ABOUT STANDING ON A STREET CORNER AND SEEING A BAPTIST CHURCH ON THIS CORNER,A METHODIST CHURCH ON THIS CORNER,A PENTACOSTAL CHURCH HERE,A CHURCH OF CHRIST HERE,PRESBYTERIAN CHURCH HERE AND A CATHOLIC CHURCH HERE ALL WITHIN WALKING DISTANCE.ALL READING THE SAME BIBLE WORSHIPPING THE SAME GOD,THE SAME SON OF GOD JESUS AND PROBABLY SINGING THE SAME SONGS. WHICH ONE OF THESE CHURCHES WILL BE IN HEAVEN? WILL WE BE DIVIDED? WILL THE WHITE PEOPLE GO HERE,BLACK PEOPLE OVER THERE,ORIENTAL PEOPLE WAY OVER THERE AND SPANISH PEOPLE WAY OVER THERE?? WILL WE PUSH ONE FOR ENGLISH,PUSH TWO FOR SPANISH? WHAT BUTTON DO WE PUSH FOR GERMAN?FRENCH? ITALIAN? HEBREW? WHAT DO WE DO IN HEAVEN? CAN WE EAT? CAN WE DRINK? CAN WE GET

MARRIED? HAVE SEX? HAVE CHILDREN? HOW OLD WILL WE BE? IF WE EAT DO WE EVENTUALLY GO TO THE BATH- ROOM? FOR RE-INCARNATION TO WORK THEN ONCE YOU DIE,YOUR PHYSICAL BODY WILL GO BACK TO MOTHER EARTH,FROM THE GROUND YOU CAME AND TO THE GROUND YOU WILL GO "ASHES TO ASHES,DUST TO DUST", YOUR SPIRIT/SOUL WILL GO TO HEAVEN AND WILL BE JUDGED. YOU WILL SEE THE TRUE TRINITY OF GOD THE FATHER,GODDESS THE MOTHER AND JESUS(YAHSHUA) ON THE RIGHT SIDE INTERCEDDING ON OUR BEHALF. YOUR WHOLE LIFE WILL FLASH BEFORE YOU AND YOU ARE JUDGED FOR WHAT YOU DID DURING THIS LIFETIME. IF YOU LIVED A GOOD LIFE THEN YOU GET TO HELP DECIDE WHAT YOU WILL DO DURING YOUR NEXT LIFETIME. HOW DO YOU KNOW WHAT IT IS LIKE DOING SOMETHING UNLESS YOU ACTUALLY EXPE- RIENCE IT. WHAT IS IT LIKE BEING ABLE TO SEE AND THEN GO BLIND UNLESS YOU ACTUALLY EXPERIENCE THAT? ON THE OTHER HAND IF YOU ARE MEAN/EVIL THEN YOU MAY BE CRIPPLED/DISESED/BLIND/DEAF OR HANDICAP FOR SINS COMMITED AND THAT WILL BE YOUR HELL GOING THRU A LIFE AS A HOMELESS PERSON OR?? YOU SEE A INNOCENT BABY BORN CRIPPLED,HANDICAPPED.BLIND OR SOME OTHER PHYS- ICAL AILMENT AND YOUR HEART CRIES OUT "WHY?" THEN YOU SEE A TEN YEAR OLD WALK UP TO A PIANO AND PLAY A MOZART SYMPHONY AND YOU SAY THAT PERSON IS GIFTED? COULD THAT PERSON BE A CON- CERT PIANIST IN A PAST LIFE? WE KNOW THRU PHYSOL- OGY AND PSYCHARITRY THAT PEOPLE DO HAVE SEVER- AL SPIRITS INSIDE THEM LIKE A DR. JEKYL AND MR. HYDE WE CALL THEM "MULTIPLE PERSONALITIES" SOME HAVE BEEN PROVEN TO HAVE AS MANY AS TEN OR MORE THIS HAS BEEN DOCUMENTED.WE HAVE THIS ABUN- DANCE OF MOVIES ABOUT GHOSTS,MEDIUMS,WITCHE S,CHARMED,WEREWOLVES AND VAMPIRES WHO CAN CHANGE THEIR HUMAN SHAPE TO DIFFERENT ANI- MALS.COULD SOME SPIRIT/SOULS BE NOT READY TO GO

TO BE JUDGED AND WANDER AROUND FOR A WHILE
UNTIL THEY ARE DIRECTED TOWARD THE LIGHT? WE
DO KNOW THAT A THIRD OF THE ORIGINAL ANGELS
WERE CAST OUT OF HEAVEN, WHERE DID THEY GO TO?
CAN THEY REPRODUCE? WE KNOW GENESIS CHAPTER
SIX TALKS ABOUT THIS SO WE KNOW THAT WE HAVE
GOOD SPIRITS AND EVIL SPIRITS ON THIS EARTH. WE
KNOW THE ORIGINAL FIRST BORN SON WAS CALLED
LUCIFER AND WAS GIVEN THE SUN TO RULE OVER. THE
ORIGINAL FIRST BORN DAUGHTER,LUCIFER'S TWIN
SISTER WAS CALLED AURIEL AND SHE WAS GIVEN THIS
EARTH TO RULE OVER. WE STILL CALL HER "MOTHER
EARTH" AND A LOT OF PEOPLE STILL WORSHIPP SATAN
AS THE "SUN" GOD WAS SATAN ONLY EVIL? NO HOW DO
YOU KNOW WHAT IS EVIL UNLESS SOMEONE TEAHES
YOU. IT IS SATAN/LUCIFER'S JOB TO TEACH YOU EVIL,IT
IS THE FATHER AND MOTHERS JOB TO TEACH YOU
GOOD.WE ARE ALL "SONS AND DAUGHTERS" AND WE
HAVE BEEN GIVEN THE POWER TO CREATE LIFE THE
SAME WAY THAT OUR FATHER AND MOTHER DID.IT IS
UP TO EACH PERSON INDIVIDUALLY TO FOLLOW WHAT
EVER PATH THEY CHOOSE. WHICH PATH DO YOU
FOLLOW? THE POWER THAT IS STRONGEST IN YOUR
LIFE IS THE POWER THAT YOU FEED THE MOST.A POWER
WILL GET LARGER OR SMALLER AS YOU FEED IT. AL-
THOUGH IT WILL NEVER COMPLETELY GO AWAY YOU
DO HAVE CONTROL OF WHAT YOU WILL FEED AND
CHOOSE NOT TO FEED. I KNOW I HAVE LIVED SEVERAL
PAST LIFETIMES,THRU MY DREAMS I REMEMBER I WAS A
MEAN,EVIL PIRATE WHO HAD TO KILL OR BE KILLED.I
WAS NOT ALWAYS THAT WAY BUT THRU A HARD LIFE
THAT WAS WHAT I NEEDED TO EXPERIENCE.EVERY LIFE-
TIME YOU WILL ONLY LIVE LONG ENOUGH TO EXPERI-
ENCE ALL THE THINGS YOU NEED TO DURING THIS
PARTICULAR LIFE,THAT MAYBE WHY SOME LIVE TO A
OLD AGE BECAUSE THEY CHOSE TO EXPERIENCE A LOT
OF THINGS OR YOUR LIFE IS VERY SHORT BECAUSE YOU
NEEDED TO EXPERIENCE A FEW THINGS.NOW LIFE

MAKES SENSE,WE UNDERSTAND WHY WE ARE HERE. WHY ARE YOU HERE? WHAT DO YOU NEED TO EXPERI- ENCE DURING THIS LIFETIME? DEEP DOWN ARE YOU JUST A LITTLE BIT VAMPYRE? DO YOU GET EXCITED THINKING YOU HAVE THIS POWER TO TAKE ENERGY FROM SOMEONE? HAVE YOU EVER HAD SEX THAT FELT SO GOOD THAT WHEN YOUR PARTNER HAD A ORGASM DID THAT EXCITE YOU? TO KNOW YOU HAVE THE POWER TO PLEASE SOMEONE ELSE AND SATIFY THEIR NEEDS. DO YOU KNOW THE ONLY WAY YOU CAN CREATE A BABY IS BOTH OF YOU HAVE TO HAVE A ORGASM? WE HAVE THE SAME GIFT OUR HEAVENLY FATHER YAHWEH AND OUR HEAVENLY MOTHER SHEKINAH USED TO CREATE THE ANGELS AND USED THIS SAME POWER TO CREATE ADAM AND EVE.WHAT DO WE DO WITH THIS POWER? DO WE HONOR OUR CREATORS WHEN WE DECIDE TO HAVE A ABORTION? THE MOST POWERFUL GIFT OUR CREATORS CAN GIVE US IS THE GIFT OF LIFE, TO BE ABLE TO CREATE LIFE WHEN WE ARE READY, BUT WE ABUSE THIS GIFT AND THEN WONDER WHY WE HAVE ALL THESE PROBLEMS. WE ARE OVER POPULATING THIS BEAUTIFUL WORLD AND SLOWLY DESTROYING IT. I JUST WONDER HOW LONG WILL THEY ALLOW IT.WE ARE CREATING SONS AND DAUGHTER AND NOT WORRIED ABOUT HOW WE CAN POSSIBLY FEED THEM. THIS FALSE ILLUSION THAT JESUS(YAHSHUA) IS THE ONLY BEGOT- TEN SON OF GOD IS ANOTHER LIE THAT MAINSTREAM RELIGION IS TELLING YOU. IF THAT IS SO, THEN WHAT ABOUT GENESIS CHAPTER SIX? STOP RIGHT NOW AND READ GENESIS CHAPTER SIX,DON'T WORRY I WILL NOT GO ANYWHERE. NOW IF MAIN STREAM RELIGION IS TELLING YOU THAT A MALE GOD,A MALE SON OF GOD AND A MALE HOLY SPIRIT ARE ONE, THEN WHO IS THE ONLY BEGOTTEN SON?HOW CAN YAHSHUA(JESUS) BE THE ONLY BEGOTTEN SON IF THEY ARE ALL ONE? HOW CAN JESUS(YAHSHUA) BE THE ONLY BEGOTTEN SON IF GENESIS WAS WRITTEN MANY YEARS BEFORE JESUS(YAHSHUA) WAS EVEN BORN?? WHAT ABOUT YOU

AND ME? ARE WE SONS AND DAUGHTERS? WHEN WE PRAY WHAT DO WE SAY? OUR FATHER WHO IS IN HEAVEN? THEN DO WE END OUR PRAYER IN JESUS(YAHSHUA) NAME? IF THEY ARE ALL ONE THEN WHY DO WE CALL THEM BY DIFFERENT NAMES? IF GOD AND JESUS (YAH-SHUA) WERE ALL ONE WHY DO WE HAVE DIFFERENT NAMES? WHY DO WE CALL OUR RELIGION CHRISTIAN? IF CHRIST AND GOD ARE ONE PERSON WHY DON'T WE CALL THEM BY THE NAME OF THE FATHER.REMEMBER GOD SAID HE WAS A JEALOUS GOD AND YOU SHALL HAVE NO GOD BEFORE HIM/ ARE WE WORSHIPPING THE SON MORE THEN THE FATHER? WE, AS A SOCIETY, THRU THE YEARS HAVE DECIDED TO ELIMINATE THE FEMALE SIDE OF GOD AND FOR A LONG TIME PEOPLE WERE PUT TO DEATH FOR THIS. WE LIVE IN A AGE WHERE NOW ITS OK TO WORSHIP AS WITCHES AND WICCA IS A BONA FIDE RELIGION AGAIN,BUT DO THEY WORSHIP BOTH IN HARMONY? NO I HAVE GONE THRU THE THREE INI-TIATIONS OF WICCA AND THEY WORSHIP THE FEMALE SIDE OF GOD USING MANY DIFFERENT NAMES AND THE MALE IS ONLY THERE TEMPORARY AS HER CONSORT,LOVER, TO PLANT THE SEED, THEN HE DIES OFF DURING THE WINTER MONTHS. DO WE HAVE BAL-ANCE? DO WE HAVE EQUALITY? DO WE HAVE HARMO-NY? MY SECOND BOOK WAS TITLED HARMONY, THE GREATEST STORY NEVER TOLD BY MELVIN ABERCROM-BIE UNDER TRAFFORD PUBLISHING. WHERE I TRIED TO CLEAR UP SOME OF THE IN-BALANCE THIS SOCIETY DID CREATE. AT THE TIME I DID NOT SHARE ALL MY VAM-PIRE QUALITIES BUT DID HINT AROUND THRU MY MANY POEMS AND PAST LIFE EXPERIENCE'S.WE HAVE FINALLY REACHED THE AGE WHERE WE CAN COME OUT OF THE PROVERBIAL CLOSET AND HIDE NO MORE. THAT IS IF YOU LIVE IN AMERICA OR THE UNITED STATES. THERE ARE STILL SOME COUNTRIES IF YOU TOLD THEM YOU ARE A WITCH OR VAMPIRE THEN THEY WOULD MAKE SURE YOU EITHER DIED OR WENT TO PRISON. A LOT OF PEOPLE IN THE LAST CENTURY WENT INTO MENTAL IN-

STITUTIONS FOR ADMITTING THEY WERE EITHER WITCHES OR VAMPIRES. DURING THE "COWBOY " DAYS OF THE OLD WEST YOU MIGHT GET HUNG OR DRAGGED BEHIND A HORSE FOR LESSER CRIMES. I FEEL A CLOSENESS TO THE NATIVE AMERICAN INDIAN. MY GRANDFATHER ON MY MOTHERS SIDE WAS RED HEADED IRISH AND HE MARRIED A FULL BLOODED CHEROKEE INDIAN. THEY SETTLED IN OKLAHOMA AND TEXAS AND HAD SIX CHILDREN TWO OF THE BOYS AND ONE OF THE GIRLS WAS DARK HAIRED,WHICH WAS MY MOM. THE OTHER TWO GIRLS AND ONE BOY WAS RED HEADED.SO WE HAD EITHER DARK HAIR OR RED HEADED KIDS. MY DADS SIDE OF THE FAMILY WAS GERMAN SO MY OLDER AND YOUNGER BROTHERS WERE BLONDE HAIR AND I WAS RED HEADED. THE GOOD PART IS NOW I COULD CALL MYSELF CELTIC,TEUTONIC OR CHEROKEE BECAUSE THE BLOODLINE OF ALL THREE WAS COURSING THRU THESE VEINS. I SOMETIMES HAVE DREAMS OF A SIMPLER LIFE BEFORE THE "WHITE MEN " STOLE OUR LAND AND MADE US WALK THE TRAIL OF TEARS,PUT US ON THEIR RESERVATIONS,TOOK AWAY OUR LANGUAGE,FORCED THEIR ENGLISH FOR US TO LEARN,FORCED THEIR FALSE RELIGIONS ON US,TOLD US WE COULD NO LONGER WORSHIP FATHER SKY AND MOTHER EARTH,KILLED OUR BUFFALO,BY THE THOUSANDS,FOR THE FUN OF IT,WHICH WAS OUR MAIN FOOD SUPPLY AND LEFT THE CARCASS TO ROT AWAY. THEN WHEN WE TRIED TO DEFEND OUR SELF THEY KILLED OUR WOMAN AND CHILDREN THEN CALLED US SAVAGE.

CHAPTER 6

THIS WILL BE CHAPTER SIX,. THIS SHORT BOOK IS
MEANT TO BE READ WITH A OPEN MIND. THE QUES-
TION YOU WILL HAVE TO EVENTUALLY ASK YOURSELF
IS, WHAT IF ALL THE THINGS HE IS SAYING IS REAL AND
THE TRUTH? IF NOT, HOW MUCH IS ACTUALLY THE
TRUTH AND WHO DECIDES ON WHAT IS THE TRUTH
AND WHAT IS FICTION? AT ONE TIME I WANTED TO
TITLE MY FIRST BOOK THE RANTINGS AND RAVINGS OF
A MAD PREACHER. INSTEAD I CHOSE THE TITLE A TEN
YOUR OLD ASKED. NOW I THINK THAT WOULD HAVE
BEEN A GOOD TITLE FOR THIS BOOK BUT I WANTED
HEAVEN, RIGHT NOW PROPHET CHRONICLES BY MELVIN
ABERCROMBIE TO BE ON THE COVER, MAYBE MY NEXT
BOOK WILL BE TITLED THE RANTINGS AND RAVINGS,
BECAUSE SOME SAY THAT IS WHAT I AM DOING. BY ME
OPENLY SAYING I AM A VAMPIRE AND HAVE LIVED OVER

2000 YEARS WOULD PUT ME IN A INSANE/MENTAL ASYLUM A HUNDRED YEARS AGO.IT WOULD ALSO BE A GOOD SELF DEFENSE IF YOU EVER COMMITED A CRIME. NOW THOUGH THEY HAVE WAYS OF TELLING IF YOU ARE JUST MAKING THINGS UP TO ACT CRAZY OR DO YOU REALLY BELIEVE THESE THINGS. I BELIEVE IF GIVEN A LIE DETECTOR TEST I WOULD ACTUALLY BELIEVE I HAVE LIVED BEFORE. I HOPE TO GIVE ENOUGH EXAMPLES FOR ANY CLEAR OPEN MINDED PERSON TO AT LEAST THINK ABOUT IT. WHO KNOWS WE MAY CREATE SOME CULT FOLLOWING AND MILLIONS OF VAMPIRES COME OUT OF THE CLOSET. WOULD THAT BE A BAD THING? AT LEAST WE CAN SEE THAT VAMPIRES DO NOT NECESSARY DRINK BLOOD, WE ARE NOT AFRAID OF THE CROSS AND DAY LIGHT DOES NOT HARM US. SPEAKING OF THE CROSS,I REMEMBER DURING THE TIME YAHSHUA CAME BACK ALIVE AND WAS ON THIS EARTH FOR AWHILE,RISEN FROM THE DEAD. HE DID NOT WANT THE SYMBOL OF THE CROSS TO BE USED IN ANY WAY TO SHOW THE PAIN AND AGONY HE WENT THRU. WHEN I DRIVE BY AND SEE A MAINSTREAM CHURCH WITH A CROSS I THINK HOW SICK ARE THEY AND WHEN I SEE A CHURCH WITH THREE CROSSES THEN THAT IS EVEN SICKER. WHAT IS WRONG WITH THIS WORLD. DO YOU NOT SEE THAT THE LAST THING THAT JESUS (YAHSHUA) WOULD WANT TO BE USED AS A SYMBOL IS A CROSS? NO ONE WHO HAS EVER DIED THAT WAY WOULD EVER WANT THAT HANGING AROUND THEIR NECK TO RE-MEMBER HOW THEY DIED BY. THIS TO ME WOULD BE SOMETHING THAT SATAN WOULD DO. I REALIZE THAT THE RULER OF THIS WORLD IS ACTUALLY LUCIFER SO THE ONLY WAY HE/SHE WILL ALLOW THIS BOOK TO BE PRINTED IS IF I PUT A GOOD WORD IN FOR THEM. THRU OUT HISTORY LUCIFER/DEVIL/SATAN,HAS BEEN GIVEN A BAD DEAL. MAJORITY OF THE SO CALLED CHRISTIAN CHURCHES TODAY, WANT TO HATE,CURSE,BIND OR IGNORE THEM.I SAY THEM BECAUSE I BELIEVE THE FIRST BORN WERE TWINS A BOY(LUCIFER) AND A TWIN

SISTER(AURIEL) AFTER THE REBELLION AND AFTER THEY WERE CAST OUT OF THE HEAVENS THEN IT WAS DECIDED THAT A WORLD WAS CREATED FOR THEM TO RULE OVER AND A SPECIES OF ANIMALS,BIRDS,FISH AND HUMANS WERE CREATED. OUR CREATORS WHICH WAS THE ORIGINAL GOD(YAHWEH) AND THE GODDESS(SHEKINAH) CREATED THE SUN FOR LUCIFER AND THE EARTH WAS NAMED AFTER MOTHER EARTH WHICH IS AURIEL. THEIR JOB IS TO RULE OVER THIS WORLD AND TEACH EVERYONE WHAT IS EVIL. HOW DO YOU KNOW WHAT IS EVIL UNLESS SOMEONE SHOWS YOU? WHAT WAS EVIL A HUNDRED YEARS AGO IS NOT EVIL NOW, WHY? HAS EVIL CHANGED? THIS IS 2009 SO A HUNDRED YEARS AGO IT WAS EVIL FOR WOMAN TO SHOW ABOVE THE KNEE BUT NOW IT IS COMMON TO SEE BIKINI CLAD WOMAN AND XXX RATED MOVIES ON TELEVISION,BUT OF COURSE IN 1909 THEY DID NOT HAVE TELEVISION. IF THERE IS SUCH A THING AS RE-INCARNATION AND YOU LIVE THIS LIFE,THEN DIE AND YOU GO TO THIS HEAVEN WHERE YOU ARE JUDGED THEN WHAT DO YOU DO? DO YOU GET TO GO TO HEAVEN? WHAT IF YOU ARE LIVING YOUR HEAVEN OR HELL RIGHT NOW? EACH LIFE YOU LIVE YOU ARE AC-COUNTABLE AND RESPONSIBLE FOR WHAT EVER YOU DID? NOW I AM SUPPOSED TO PUT IN A GOOD WORD FOR OUR RULERS SO HOW DO YOU KNOW WHAT IS GOOD OR EVIL UNLESS SOMEONE TEACHES YOU? WHO CREATED LUCIFER AND AURIEL? THE SAME PERSON WHO CREATED EVERYTHING SO IF LUCIFER IS EVIL THE THE PERSON WHO CREATED HIM HAS TO BE EVIL,SO IF YOU CURSE THE DEVIL DO YOU NOT CURSE THE PERSON WHO CREATED THE DEVIL? IF YOU BIND THE DEVIL OR HATE THE DEVIL DO YOU NOT BIND AND.OR HATE THE PERSON WHO CREATED THE DEVIL? REMEMBER THEIR ARE TWO FORCES OUT THEIR,GOOD AND EVIL,HOW DID WE GET TWO FORCES? IF WE LOOK AT THE FIRST WISDOM IT IS DUALITY WHICH USES A COIN TO SHOW THATEVERYTHINGHASTWOSIDES,SOMALE/FEMALE,UP/

DOWN,FORWARD/BACKWARDS,LEFT/RIGHT, GOOD/ EVIL,ETC. JUST SHOWS THE DUALITY OF EVERYTHING. CAN A MALE CREATE LIFE BY HIS SELF? NO CAN A FEMALE CREATE LIFE BY HER SELF? NO IT TAKES BOTH IN PER-FECT LOVE IN PERFECT TRUST WHETHER IT IS HUMANS,ANIMALS,BIRDS OR FISH,THIS IS THE WAY OF ALL CREATION,WE CAN ARGUE TILL THE COWS COME HOME OR ONE OF US IS BLUE IN THE FACE BUT SIMPLE COMMON SENSE AND THAT GOOD OLE GUT FEELING TELLS US THE REAL TRUTH. YOU CAN WRITE 15 BOOKS ABOUT WHAT EVER TOPIC YOU WANT TO BUT THAT DOES NOT MAKE IT TRUE. ITS THE SAME WITH THIS BOOK, WHAT MAKES IT TRUE? ONLY YOU CAN DECIDE. USE SIMPLE LOGIC AND GUT FEELING,COMMON SENSE TELLS YOU THE REALITY.LUCIFER IS THE RULER OF THIS WORLD WHETHER YOU ARE WILLING TO ACCEPT IT OR NOT DOES NOT MATTER. YOU CAN STICK YOUR HEAD IN THE SAND AND HOPE IT WILL GO AWAY BUT IT WILL NOT. THE AVERAGE PERSON WILL ONLY REMEMBER 20% OF WHAT THEY READ SO I WILL ASK YOU TO READ THIS BOOK OVER AND OVER. SOME OF YOU WILL THROW IT AWAY BECAUSE YOU ARE NOT READY FOR THE TRUTH BUT ITS THE TRUTH THAT WILL SET YOU FREE. SO YOU WILL KEEP ON LIVING THIS LIFE,SAY 50,60,80 YEARS WHAT ARE YOU DOING WITH THIS LIFE YOU ARE LIVING RIGHT NOW? ARE YOU WASTING IT? WAITING TO DIE, THEN HOPE YOU EITHER GET TO GO TO HEAVEN OR BURN IN HELL FOREVER AND EVER? IS THIS THE ONLY TWO CHOICES? WHAT ARE YOU GOING TO DO IN HEAVEN? CAN YOU EAT? DRINK? HOW OLD WILL YOU BE? CAN YOU GET MARRIED? HAVE CHILDREN? WILL YOU BE A MALE OR FEMALE? BLACK,WHITE BROWN OR YELLOW? WHAT IF ONE LIFE YOU ARE A TYPICAL WHITE MIDDLE CLASS MALE WHO LIVED TO BE 87,BORN IN AMERICA,MARRIED 3 CHILDREN 7 GRANDCHILDREN,LIVED A GOOD FAIR LIFE THEN YOUR NEXT LIFE YOU CHOOSE TO BE BORN IN RUSSIA AS A LOWER CLASS FEMALE SO YOU HAVE TO GO BACK INTO

THE WOMB TO LEARN A DIFFERENT SET OF
CUSTOMS,CULTURE,LANGUAGE AND LIFESTYLE? ON
THE OTHER HAND WHAT IF YOU WERE EVIL AND DID A
LOT OF BAD THINGS DURING THIS LIFE TIME SO YOU
DO NOT GET TO HELP CHOOSE SO THEN YOU ARE BORN
AS A POOR HOMELESS,HANDICAP PERSON LIVING IN
SOME FAR AWAY VILLAGE WAKING UP HUNGARY AND
GOING TO BED HUNGARY? THE HEBREW/JEWISH TYPE
PEOPLE HAD NO PROBLEM KNOWING ABOUT RE-IN-
CARNATION, THEY ACCEPTED IT AND UNDERSTOOD
THAT IS WHY SOME PEOPLE ARE SICK,DISEASE,HANDIC
AP,BLIND,DEAF,ETC. THEY DID NOT LIKE THE IDEA OF
JESUS(YAHSHUA) GOING AROUND HEALING THEM.
WHAT THE AVERAGE CHRISTIAN CHURCH FAILS TO RE-
ALIZE IS THAT JESUS(YAHSHUA) IS THE REAL SON OF
GOD AND THIS FALSE DOCTRINE OF A TRINITY IS ALL
WRONG. YES THEIR IS A TRINITY BUT IT IS THE
FATHER(YAHWEH), THE SON(YAHSHUA) AND THE
FEMALE SIDE OF GOD AS THE HOLY SPIRIT(SHEKINAH)
DID YOU KNOW THE ORIGINAL HEBREW LANGUAGE
NEVER HAD THE LETTER J IN IT? SO WHAT WE CALL AS A
ENGLISH VERSION OF THE SONS NAME CAME ABOUT
AROUND KING JAMES TIME WHICH ADDED THE LETTER
J TO THE ENGLISH ALAPHABET. SO DURING THE LIFE OF
YAHSHUA HE WAS A GOOD HEBREW/JEWISH PERSON
WHO NEVER WORSHIPPED HIS HEAVENLY FATHER GOD
OR MOTHER,GODDESS ON SUNDAY. HE NEVER ATE
PORK,CATFISH,SHRIMP OR LOBSTER. HE KEPT THE
KOSHER FOOD LAWS, READ ALL OF MATTHEW CHAPTER
FIVE ESPECIALLY THE LAST PART. ASK ANY HEBREW/
JEWISHPERSONWHOEVERSTUDIEDTHEKABBALAH,THE
TREE OF LIFE AND THEY WILL SHOW THAT THE FEMALE
SIDE IS CALLED THE BINAH(WOMB) OR SHEKINAH,THE
FEMALE SIDE OF GOD. OF COURSE JUST LIKE WE CAN
COME UP WITH A 100 NAMES TO CALL OUR HEAVENLY
FATHER I AM SURE WE CAN COME UP WITH A LOT OF
NAMES TO CALL OUR MOTHER.PART OF A STORY I WISH
TO SHARE WITH YOU COMES FROM A ELDERS COVEN

GROUP. I DO NOT KNOW THE AUTHOR BUT I WILL QUOTE SO PEOPLE WILL KNOW THIS DID NOT COME FROM ME. " I AM PART OF THE WHOLE OF NATURE. THE ROCKS, THE ANIMALS, THE PLANTS,THE ELEMENTS ARE MY RELATIVES. OTHER HUMANS ARE MY SISTERS AND BROTHERS,WHATEVER THEIR RACES,OR COLOR. THE EARTH IS MY MOTHER AND THE SKY IS MY FATHER, I AM A PART OF THIS LARGE FAMILY OF NATURE,NOT THE MASTER OF IT. I HAVE MY OWN SPECIAL PART TO PLAY AS I LIVE THIS LIFE." WHEN I LIVED THE LIFE OF A CHERO-KEE INDIAN THIS WAS MY BELIEF SYSTEM. WE GOT AWAY FROM MOTHER NATURE AND WE CHOP DOWN HER TREES AND RAVAGE THE LAND AND DUMP OUR SEWER AND GARBAGE LIKE THEIR WILL BE NO TOMORROW. THEN WE WONDER WHY MOTHER EARTH IS FIGHTING BACK.WHY DO WE HAVE TORNADOES AND FLOOD.TO HELP PURIFY AND CLEAN THE MESS WE CREATED. LOOK AT WHAT HAPPENED TO LOUISIANA,IN THE FIRST PLACE MOST WAS CREATED UNDER SEA LEVEL.THE WHOLE TOWN OF NEW ORLEANS IS FIVE FOOT UNDER SEA LEVEL THAT TELLS ME ITS JUST A MATTER OF TIME. DOES ANYONE IN LOUISIANA KEEP THE KOSHER FOOD LAWS? DOES ANYONE KEEP THE SEVENTH DAY SABBATH? DID THEY CHANGE THEIR WAYS? NO, THEY ARE STILL DOING THE SAME THING. DON'T WORRY THE GOVERN-MENT WILL SOLVE YOUR PROBLEMS. GO AHEAD AND EAT ALL THIS SCAVENGER FOOD,GO AHEAD AND DO WHAT YOU WANT TO, THE MAIN CHURCH AROUND THEIR IS CATHOLIC SO JUST DRINK,EAT PARTY SIX DAYS AND GIVE SOME OF YOUR MONEY ON SUNDAY,THE FIRST DAY OF THE WEEK AND IF YOU GO TO CHURCH ON SUNDAY NIGHT DON'T WORRY THAT IS ACTUALLY THE SECOND DAY BUT DON'T WORRY WE ARE SAVED BY GRACE AND NOT UNDER THE OLD LAW.JUST CONFESS YOUR SINS TO THE CATHOLIC FATHER AND HE WILL TELL YOU TO DO SO MANY "HELL MARY'S" AND YOU WILL BE OK,DON'T WORRY ABOUT THE 40,60,80 YEARS YOU ARE LIVING NOW IT DON'T MEAN NOTHING.

CHAPTER 7

THIS WILL BE THE SEVENTH CHAPTER. I REALIZE I WILL MAKE A LOT OF PEOPLE MAD AT ME,ESPECIALLY THE JEWISH FAITH. I AM NOT WRITING THIS BOOK TO GET PEOPLE MAD AT ME BUT TO EXPOSE THE REAL TRUTH. HOW MANY PEOPLE WHO READ THIS ACTUALLY BE- LIEVES THAT I AM A VAMPIRE? DID YOU KNOW YOU CAN GO TO YOUR COMPUTER AND LOOK UP TEMPLE OF THE VAMPIRE, BACK IN 1989 I WENT THRU THE INITIATIONS OF PREDATOR BIBLE, PRIESTHOOD BIBLE AND SORCERY BIBLE.I ALSO REMAINED ACTIVE THRU THE YEAR 2002 BY THE LIFEFORCE,WHICH IS A PUBLICATION THAT CHANGES THE PASSWORD. MY LAST COPY IS OF JULY 2002 AND THE NEW CABAL PASSWORD THEN WAS MINO- TAUR. I GOT MARRIED AGAIN AT THIS TIME AND MY NEW WIFE, A GOOD LITTLE CATHOLIC GIRL, DID NOT UNDERSTAND ME WORSHIPPING VAMPIRES AND READ-

ING ABOUT WICCA SO I WENT UNDERGROUND FOR
AWHILE AGAIN. IT TOOK ME THIS MANY YEARS TO CON-
VINCE HER THAT I AM NOT COMPLETELY CRAZY JUST
HALF CRAZY WILL SUFFICE FOR NOW, THIS WAS ALL
CALLED DEVIL WORSHIP BUT IN REALITY WHO CREAT-
ED THE DEVIL? IF OUR GOD YAHWEH AND OUR GOD-
DESS SHEKINAH CREATED EVERYTHING THEN THEY
HAD TO CREATE LUCIFER/SATAN/DEVIL. IF THE DEVIL
WAS AROUND TO TEMPT EVE AND BEEN AROUND FROM
THE BEGINNING THEN WHERE DOES JESUS(YAHSHUA)
FIT IN? WHO CREATED GOOD AND EVIL? WHY DO WE
HAVE CHOICES? DO WE GET TO DECIDE WHO WE WANT
TO FOLLOW? BUT THEN IF WE DO NOT FOLLOW GOD
THEN WE ARE PUNISHED? IF YOU WILL REMEMBER
WHAT HAPPENED IN THE BOOK OF JOB. THE DEVIL/
SATAN TOLD YAHWEH HE COULD MAKE JOB HATE AND
CURSE HIM,SO GOD ALLOWED SATAN TO GIVE IT HIS
BEST SHOT. WE ALL KNOW WHAT HAPPENED, JOB
PROVED FAITHFUL. SO WHAT IF SATAN DID THE SAME
THING WITH MOSES? SATAN,WHO IS THE RULER OF
THIS WORLD ANYWAY CONVINCES HIS FATHER, OUR
YAHWEH, TO GET HIS PEOPLE TO FOLLOW HIM AND
NOT ONLY FOLLOW HIM BUT CHANGE WHAT OUR CRE-
ATOR MADE? SO GOD ALLOWS SATAN TO AGAIN, GIVE IT
YOUR BEST SHOT. SO EVERYONE KNOWS WHEN YOU
THINK ABOUT A FIRE THEN YOU AUTOMATICALLY
THINK OF HELL OR HADES THE BOTTOMLESS PIT THAT
THE SO CALLED CHRISTIANS SAY YOU WILL GO WHEN
YOU DIE IF YOU BEEN A BAD BOY.WE ALSO KNOW THAT
GOD CHANGED SATAN,AKA LUCIFER/DEVIL INTO A
SNAKE.SO IF SOMEONE COMES ALONG AND USES THE
SYMBOL OF FIRE OR A SNAKE THEN THE FIRST THING
THAT COMES TO MY MIND IS EVIL OR DEVIL/LUCIFER.
SOMEHOW MOSES MISTOOK THIS TO REPRESENT THE
YAHWEH CREATOR GOD BUT IF GOD WAS TRYING TO
TALK TO MOSES WOULD HE USE A FIRE OR SNAKE AS A
SYMBOL TO SHOW MOSES THIS IS COMING FROM THE
CREATOR GOD AND NOT COMING FROM LUCIFER/

SATAN?? WE KNOW LONG BEFORE THIS WORLD WAS CREATED WE HAD A REBELLION WHERE A THIRD OF THE ANGELS WERE CAST OUT OF HEAVEN. WHERE DID THEY GO? FIRST ASK YOURSELF WHY WAS THIS WORLD CREATED IN THE FIRST PLACE? COULD THIS WORLD BE CREATED TO GIVE THE FALLEN ANGELS THEIR OWN PLACE TO RULE? WAS ADAM AND HIS SONS EVER CIRCUMSICED? WHAT ABOUT NOAH AND ALL HIS SONS? WHY WOULD OUR CREATOR GOD CREATE US IN HIS IMAGE AND FOR THOUSANDS OF YEARS LEAVE IT THIS WAY THEN OUT OF THE BLUE SAY IF YOU WANT TO BE MY PEOPLE AND FOLLOW ME THEN YOU NEED TO CUT YOUR FORESKIN OFF OF YOUR HEAD OF YOUR PENIS AND MARK YOURSELF SO I WILL KNOW YOU ARE MY PEOPLE AND EVERYONE ELSE ARE NOT. I WILL USE THE SYMBOL OF A BURNING BUSH TO SHOW YOU I AM YOUR GOD AND YOU WILL BOW DOWN TO ME. I ALSO WILL TELL YOU TO LAY YOUR STAFF DOWN AND I WILL TURN IT INTO A LARGE SNAKE THAT WILL CONSUME ANY OTHER SNAKE TO SHOW YOU I AM THE GOD OF THIS WORLD. THE CRAZY THING IS THE HEBREW PEOPLE FELL FOR IT.WHAT WAS GOD DOING WHILE ALL THIS WAS HAPPENING? IF GOD HAS THE POWER TO CREATE A FLOOD AND DESTROY THIS WORLD THEN DOES HIS FIRST BORN SON,LUCIFER HAVE ANY POWER? COULD LUCIFER DO ALL THESE TRICKS,THE PARTING OF THE WATERS,ETC.? IF GOD ALLOWS HIS FIRST BORN SON TO RULE THIS WORLD AND STEPS BACK TO SEE WHAT THESE PEOPLE HE CREATED WOULD DO. IF GOD KNEW EVERYTHING WOULD HE NOT KNOW THAT ADAM AND EVE WOULD EAT THE FORBIDDEN FRUIT? WOULD HE NOT KNOW THAT CAIN WOULD KILL HIS BROTHER ABEL? GOD IS SUPPOSED TO KNOW THE HAIRS ON YOUR HEAD,THEN HE MUST ALSO KNOW THAT EVERYDAY YOUR BODY CHANGES,CELLS GROW AND DIE ALL THE TIME NEW HAIR GROWS AND OLD HAIR FALLS OUT. I AM NOT SAYING THESE THINGS TO MAKE FUN OF GOD. I BELIEVE THAT THEIR IS NOT ONLY A MALE GOD BUT

ALSO A FEMALE GODDESS, WE WILL TALK ABOUT THAT. LONG BEFORE THE CHRISTIANS, JEWISH, ISLAM, BUDDAH, HINDU, ETC RELIGIONS. IN THE BEGINNING WE HAD ONE CHURCH, ONE RELIGION AND WE ALL SPOKE ONE LANGUAGE. I BELIEVE THAT ONE LANGUAGE WAS HEBREW. THEY WERE THE CHOSEN PEOPLE. SO THAT WOULD MEAN THAT ADAM AND EVE WERE BASICALLY HEBREW TYPE PEOPLE. WE ALSO BELIEVE THAT NOAH, HIS WIFE, AND THEIR CHILDREN WERE ALL OF THE HEBREW FAITH. BEFORE I GO ANY FARTHER, LET ME SAY ONE THING DO NOT BELIEVE ANY WORD I SAY OR ANY OTHER PREACHER, TEACHER ETC. UNLESS THEY CAN PROVE IT TO YOU. SO MAKE ME PROVE IT TO YOU. TO ME THERE ARE THREE WAYS TO PROVE ANYTHING. FIRST, SHOW ME WHERE IT IS WRITTEN IN THE BIBLE. ANY PERSON TELLING YOU ANYTHING MAKE THEM SHOW YOU, YOU HAVE A RIGHT TO SEE AND UNDERSTAND. SECOND, WE KNOW THAT EVERYTHING EVER WRITTEN ABOUT JESUS (YAHSHUA) COULD NOT BE PUT IN JUST ONE BOOK SO WE KNOW THEIR ARE OTHER BOOKS, SOME CALLED THE LOST BOOKS OF THE BIBLE, THE FORGOTTEN BOOKS, THE DEAD SEA SCROLLS, THE NAG HAMMADI, ETC. BUT MOST OF ALL THE THIRD WAY IS GOOD OLD COMMON SENSE. THAT GUT FEELING WHEN SOMEONE TELLS YOU SOMETHING, DOES IT JUST MAKE SENSE? WE KNOW THRU OUT THE BIBLE AND OTHER WORKS THE STORY TELLER WOULD USE PARABLES TO TEACH. SOME WOULD UNDERSTAND, OTHERS WERE NOT READY AND DID NOT UNDERSTAND. ONE STORY I WANT TO SHARE IS IF YOU CAN IMAGINE THAT EVERYONE IN THE WHOLE WORLD IS ON THIS GIANT CIRCULAR STAIRCASE SLOWLY GOING AROUND AND AROUND. SLOWLY GOING UP. IT DOES NOT MATTER WHAT STEP YOU ARE ON, THERE MAYBE THOUSANDS OF OTHER PEOPLE ON THE SAME STEP YOU ARE ON. YOU CAN COME BACK TWO YEARS FROM NOW AND SEE SOME PEOPLE ARE STILL ON THE SAME STEP. THEY ARE HAPPY AND SATISFIED WHERE THEY ARE AT. THERE IS

NOTHING WRONG WITH THAT. SOME PEOPLE CAN LOOK UP AND SEE OTHERS ON THE NEXT STEP HIGHER. HOW DID THEY GET UP TO THAT NEXT STEP? WHAT DID THEY DO TO CLIMB UP TO THAT NEXT STEP? THEY CAN ALSO LOOK DOWN AND SEE A LOT OF BROTHERS AND SISTERS THAT ARE ON A LOWER STEP, WHY? SO AS YOU GO THRU YOUR DAILY LIFE YOU CAN AND WILL MEET OTHER PEOPLE AND SOMETIMES,NOW, YOU MIGHT IMAGINE WHAT STEP THAT PERSON IS ON. ARE THEY HIGHER UP THEN YOU ARE? ARE THEY ON A LOWER STEP THEN YOU? WHAT CAN YOU DO TO BRING THAT PERSON UP? WHAT CAN YOU DO TO BRING YOURSELF UP ONE STEP? THIS IS PART OF THE FIRST LESSON IF WE CAN IMAGINE THAT ONE DAY WE WILL DIE,OUR HUMAN BODY WILL GO BACK TO THE GROUND,WE KNOW THIS,OUR SPIRIT/SOUL WILL GO TO HEAVEN TO BE JUDGED, RIGHT? NOW ONCE YOU ARE UP IN HEAVEN THE FIRST LESSON YOU WILL SEE IS THAT, IN THE BE-GINNING THERE WAS ONE CHURCH,ONE RELIGION,AND ALL SPOKE ONE LANGUAGE AND NOW THERE IS STILL ONE CHURCH,ONE RELIGION AND THEY ALL SPEAK ONE LANGUAGE. WHAT THAT MEANS IS WHEN YOU GET TO HEAVEN THERE WILL NOT BE BAPTIST HERE, METH-ODIST OVER THERE,PENTACOST OVER THERE, CHURCH OF CHRIST OVER THERE, CATHOLICS OVER THERE,NON DENOMINATIONS OVER THERE, ISLAM OVER THERE,JEWISH PEOPLE OVER THERE, BUDDAH BELIEV-ERS WAY OVER THERE,HINDU BELIEVERS OVER THERE,ETC.THE SAME WITH PEOPLE THERE WILL NOT BE WHITE PEOPLE HERE,BLACK PEOPLE OVER THERE,BROWN PEOPLE OVER THERE,YELLOW PEOPLE WAY OVER THERE,ETC. THERE WILL NOT BE PUSH ONE FOR ENGLISH,PUSH TWO FOR SPANISH, PUSH THREE FOR FRENCH,PUSH FOUR FOR ITALIAN,PUSH FIVE FOR GREEK,ETC.ONCE WE REALIZE THAT WE ARE SCAT-TERED AND CONFUSED AND WE HAVE NO POWER,WE REALIZE THAT ALL THESE PEOPLE WHO ARE TRYING TO JOIN US TOGETHER IS NOT THE ANTI-CHRIST AFTER

ALL. SATAN WANTS YOU TO BE DIVIDE,HE KNOWS YOU HAVE NO POWER AS LONG AS HE KEEPS YOU SCATTERED AND CONFUSED.FORGET EVERYTHING ELSE AND RE-MEMBER THE GOOD OLD GUT FEELING? UNITED WE STAND DIVIDED WE FALL??WE CAN LET PEOPLE TELL US THAT IF WE GO TO THIS ONE WORLD GOVERNMENT THEN THAT IS EVIL? IN THE BEGINNING OUR CREATORS DECIDED TO CREATE THIS PERFECT GARDEN OF EDEN. MAN AND WOMAN WERE CREATED IN "OUR IMAGE IN THE IMAGE OF US". CAN WE EVER GO BACK TO THIS PERFECT GARDEN OF EDEN? WHAT DO WE,AS A SOCI-ETY NEED TO DO? BY FOLLOWING THIS FIRST SIMPLE LESSON DOES THAT BRING US CLOSER TO OUR CRE-ATORS? CAN EVERYTHING BE AS SIMPLE AS FIVE BASIC SIMPLE LESSONS? YOU CAN GET 10 PEOPLE OFF THE STREET AND PUT THEM IN A ROOM AND PROBABLY GET 11 DIFFERENT OPINIONS.IS THIS NORMAL? YES YOU CAN GO TO YOUR TYPICAL CHRISTIAN CHURCH SERVICE AND WHAT IS THE DIFFERENCE? THEY WILL READ THE SAME BIBLE,WORSHIP THE SAME FATHER,WORSHIP THE SAME SON,SING A LOT OF THE SAME SONGS,STICK THIS OFFERING PLATE IN FRONT OF YOUR FACE AND JUDGE YOU BY HOW MUCH YOU GIVE THEM.ONE DAY OF THE WEEK THEY DRESS UP TALK ABOUT WHO DIDN'T SHOW UP AND THE OTHER DAYS GO BACK AND DO WHAT EVER THEY WANT TO. THEN WONDER WHY WE HAVE SO MANY DISEASES,SICKNESS,CANCER,PROBLEMS,ILLNESS. WE ARE NOT SATISFIED,NOT HAPPY,WE SEARCH FROM CHURCH TO CHURCH,JOB TO JOB,RELATIONSHIP TO ANOTHER RELATIONSHIP,ETC.WHAT IS THE ANSWERS? WHY ARE WE HERE? DO WE HAVE A PURPOSE IN LIFE? WHAT WOULD THE REAL JESUS DO? WE KNOW THAT THE REAL JESUS WAS BORN AS A HEBREW JEWISH TYPE PERSON.WE KNOW HE LIVED AROUND 33 YEARS ON THIS EARTH.WE ALSO KNOW DURING THAT 33 YEARS THERE WAS NO NEW TESTAMENT. THIS WAS NOT CRE-ATED UNTIL LONG AFTER HE DIED. THE FIRST BOOK WRITTEN WAS FROM MARK AROUND 49 AD THIS WOULD

BE AROUND 15 YEARS AFTER HE DIED. MOST OF THE NEW TESTAMENT,WE KNOW WAS WRITTEN AROUND 60AD THRU 90AD. WE ALOS KNOW THAT PAUL NEVER MET JESUS,ORIGINALLY PAUL WAS CALLED SAUL AND HE WAS A BOUNTY HUNTER LOOKING FOR CHRISTIANS,CAPTURING THEM AND TURNING THEM IN.THEN WE KNOW THE LAST BOOKS WRITTEN WERE FROM JOHN WHO DID KNOW JESUS(YAHSHUA) AROUND 85-90AD.THE RAINBOW BIBLE IS A GOOD VERSION THAT TELLS A LOT OF LITTLE THINGS ABOUT THE WRITERS. MY MAIN BIBLE IS THE GOOD OLD KING JAMES VERSION I RECIEVED FROM LIBERTY UNIVERSITY,JERRY FALWELLS SCHOOL.I ALSO ATTENDED SUMMIT SCHOOL OF THEOLOGY IN DENVER COLORADO. I AM THE AUTHOR OF TWO BOOKS UNDER TRAFFORD PUBLISHING AND MY NAME MELVIN ABERCROMBIE. I WROTE 20 POEMS UNDER WWW.POETRY.COM . WE DON'T NEED ANOTHER CHURCH. JUST IN THE AREA WE LIVE WHICH IS HUNT COUNTY TEXAS WE HAVE OVER 100 CHURCHES. WHICH ONE IS RIGHT? WHICH ONE IS WRONG? MOST PREACHERS MEAN WELL THEIR INTENTIONS ARE GOOD. I GREW UP AS A BAPTIST. A LOT OF MY FAMILY ARE STILL BAPTIST.AFTER READING THE BIBLE AND TALKING TO OUR GOD I REALIZED SOME OF THE SIMPLE TRUTHS. WHAT GOOD ARE THE TRUTHS IF YOU DON'T SHARE THEM? DON'T GET ME WRONG FOR ANY CHURCH TO GROW IT WILL TAKE A LOT OF PEOPLE AND A LOT OF MONEY.WE UNDERSTAND THE LAW OF GIVING YOUR TITHES AND OFFERINGS. WE SIMPLY PUT THE OFFERING BOX IN A CORNER OUT OF THE WAY. THOSE WHO FEEL BLESSED AND WANT TO CONTRIBUTE TO THE MINISTRY CAN WITHOUT A OFFERING PLATE BEING SHOVED IN YOUR FACE. WE DO NOT WANT TO KICK ANYONE OUT OF THE CHURCH MINISTRY. WE NEED PREACHERS,WE NEED TEACHERS,DEACONS AND ELDERS,SONG LEADERS AND MUSICIANS.LISTEN TO THE FIVE LESSONS THEN DECIDE FOR YOUR SELF.I PROMISE YOU THAT YOU WILL NEVER BE THE SAME PERSON. ASK QUESTIONS,EXPECT AN-

SWERS. DO NOT TAKE ANYTHING FOR GRANTED JUST BECAUSE SOMEONE SAID SO. THE ONLY STUPID QUESTION IS THE ONE YOU NEVER ASKED. REMEMBER WE ARE ALL ON DIFFERENT STEPS. WHAT DO WE NEED TO BRING EVERYONE A LITTLE CLOSER? WE ARE ALL BROTHERS AND SISTERS IN THE CHURCH.LOOK AROUND AT THIS WORLD THAT WE,AS A SOCIETY, HAVE CREATED. IS THIS WHAT YOU WANT YOUR CHILDREN AND GRANDCHILDREN TO BE INVOLVED IN?THIS WORLD DID NOT HAPPEN OVER NIGHT. IT TOOK US MANY YEARS TO GET THIS WAY AND IT WILL TAKE US A WHILE TO CHANGE. WHAT ARE YOU WILLING TO DO? YOU HAVE TO STAND FOR SOMETHING OR YOU WILL FALL FOR ANYTHING.IT REALLY DOES NOT BOTHER ME WHAT YOU THINK.IT DOES NOT BOTHER ME IF YOU CHOOSE NOT TO READ THIS BOOK OR HEED ITS APPLICATIONS. THAT IS YOUR CHOICE. I DO KNOW THAT I AM TEMPORARY STUCK IN THIS BODY FOR NOW. I AM A VERY OLD SPIRIT/SOUL WHO HAPPENS TO BE TEMPORARY STUCK IN THIS PHYSICAL BODY SO I CAN EAT,DRINK AND SURVIVE. I DO KNOW THAT I WILL LIVE MANY MORE LIFE TIMES UNLESS THIS WORLD ENDS OR JESUS(YAHSHUA) DECIDES TO RETURN. ONE OF MY DREAMS WAS ABOUT A LARGE TABLE WITH A HUNDRED EYEBALLS,ALL VARIOUS SIZE'S COMING FROM VARIOUS HUMANS,ANIMALS FISH AND BIRDS. I ASKED WHAT DOES ALL THIS MEAN? A VOICE SAID REMEMBER WHEN YOU WERE IN HIGH SCHOOL AND COLLEGE YOU STUDIED BIOLOGY,PHYSICAL SCIENCE,ETC.? YES I REPLIED, THEN REMEMBER THE TEST THAT YOU HAD TO DESCRIBE THE DIFFERENT PARTS OF THE EYEBALL? I REMEMBER THE RETINA, THE PUPIL, THE IRIS, THE CORNEA,THEN THE VOICE SAID, WHICH EYEBALL IS HUMAN? WHICH EYEBALL DOES NOT HAVE ALL THESE THINGS?.IF YOU REMEMBER THE ATOM AND MOLECULES THEN THERE IS THE PROTRON,ELECTRON.AND NEUTRON. HOW MANY ATOMS AND MOLECULES DOES IT TAKE TO CREATE ONE EYEBALL? DO WE, AS HUMANS HAVE SOMETHING IN

COMMON WITH OUR ANIMAL BROTHERS AND SISTERS? DO WE AS HUMANS HAVE SOMETHING IN COMMON WITH OUR BIRD,BROTHERS AND SISTERS? DO WE, AS HUMAN HAVE ANYTHING IN COMMON WITH OUR FISH,BROTHERS AND SISTERS? DO WE ONLY HAVE THE EYEBALL AS COMMON? WHAT ABOUT HEARING? RE-MEMBER THE TEST? REMEMBER THE PARTS OF A EAR? THE CANAL? THE HAMMER,STIRRUP AND THE EAR DRUM? DOES A COW,A HORSE,A DOG,CAT ETC. NOT HAVE THE SAME? ARE THEY MORE IN COMMON? DO WE HAVE TWO EYES TO SEE AND TWO EARS TO HEAR?.IF YOU TAKE A BRAIN OUT AND CUT IT OPEN WILL YOU FIND SIMILARITIES? WHAT ABOUT A LUNG? A HEART? DIGESTIVE TRACT AND REPRODUCTIVE ORGANS? BONES? MUSCLE? VEINS AND ARTERIES? WE ARE NOT ALONE WHEN WE WERE CREATED IN THE IMAGE OF OUR GOD AND GODDESS ALMOST ALL OF THEIR CRE-ATION HAS THIS SAME THREAD THAT HOLDS US ALL TOGETHER.THE ONLY DIFFERENCE BETWEEN ME,AS A HUMAN AND A GORILLA,AS A ANIMAL IS SO MANY ATOMS AND MOLECULES THEN EVERY ANIMAL,BIRD AND FISH CAN BE BROKEN DOWN INTO SO MANY MOLECULES,SO MANY ATOMS,SO MANY PROTRONS,SO MANY ELECTRONS,ETC. SOMETHING TO THINK ABOUT?? UNTIL THEN SHALOM

CHAPTER 8

THIS WILL BE THE EIGHTH CHAPTER,HOW DO I PROVE
RE-INCARNATION. SO YOU THINK MAYBE AFTER READ-
ING THIS FAR,MAYBE YOU HAVE LIVED IN A PAST LIFE?
HOW DO I PROVE IT? HOW DO I CONVINCE MY SELF
THAT ALL YOU ARE SAYING IS A LIE OR THE TRUTH?.
IN REALITY, AS A VAMPIRE,AND AS A WATCHER, I HAVE
ALREADY GONE THRU THESE TEST AND IF I CAN DO
THEM THEN ANYONE SHOULD HAVE A LITTLE SUCESS.
REMEMBER EVERYONE IS DIFFERENT. DEEP DOWN IN
YOUR BRAIN YOU HAVE UNDER ALL THE COBWEBS,
PART OF THE PAST LIFE YOU HAVE LIVED. MOST OF THE
TIME YOU CHOOSE TO FORGET THEM SO YOU HAVE
TO WORK TO GET THEM BACK OUT.YOU HAVE TO ASK
YOUR SELF, ARE YOU READY TO FIND OUT? WHAT IF YOU
FIND OUT YOUR PAST LIFE YOU WERE A EVIL PERSON?
DO YOU REALLY WANT TO KNOW? INSTEAD OF READ-

ING A BUNCH OF BOOKS ON RE-INCARNATION,WHICH
IS GOOD AND I DO RECCOMEND IT, YOU CAN DO THIS
SIMPLE SELF HYPNOSIS PREFERABLE BY YOUR SELF OR
WITH SOMEONE YOU TRUST. STEP ONE, HAVE YOU
EVER DONE ANY RELAXING MEDITATION BREATHING?
FIRST YOU CLOSE YOUR EYES,BE IN A ROOM WITH NO
NOISE,DISCONNECT THE TELEPHONE AND ANYTHING
ELSE THAT WILL INTERRUPT YOU. BREATHE IN WITH A
COUNT TO FOUR,HOLD THE BREATHE WITH A COUNT
TO FOUR, THEN EXHALE WITH A COUNT TO FOUR. GET
IN THE HABIT OF BREATHING THIS WAY, AFTER AWHILE
YOU NO LONGER HAVE TO COUNT TO FOUR YOU AU-
TOMATICALLY KNOW TO BREATHE IN,HOLD, THEN
EXHALE. IF YOU HAVE SOME BAD HABITS, YOU CAN TELL
YOURSELF AS YOU BREATHE IN, ONLY GOOD THINGS
WILL COME INTO ME,YOU CAN IMAGINE BREATHING
IN A WHITE PURE LIGHT AND AS YOU HOLD YOUR
BREATHE, YOU ARE IMAGINING ALL THE THINGS YOU
WANT TO CHANGE IN YOUR LIFE AND AS YOU EXHALE
YOU ARE PUSHING ALL THE EVIL,BAD THINGS OUT OF
YOUR BODY. AFTER YOU DO THIS FOR AWHILE AND FEEL
COMFORTABLE, RELAXED. THEN IMAGINE YOU SEE THIS
LARGE OAK TREE.THIS OAK TREE IS SO LARGE THAT
THREE PEOPLE CAN BARELY PUT THEIR ARMS AROUND
THIS TREE. YOU LOOK UP AND SEE ALL THE BRANCHES
AND LIMBS AND CAN SEE ALL THE ANIMALS AND BIRDS
THAT ARE LIVING IN THIS HUGE OAK TREE. OUT OF RE-
SPECT YOU HONOR THIS TREE AND CALL HIM FATHER
OAK,AS YOU BOW DOWN,YOU ASK FATHER OAK TO GIVE
TELL YOU ABOUT YOUR SELF. AS YOU WALK AROUND
THIS TREE YOU NOTICE A DOOR WITH YOUR FULL NAME
AT BIRTH, YOUR BIRTHDAY AND YOUR ZODIAC SIGN
YOU WERE BORN UNDER. YOU OPEN THIS DOOR TO SEE
A STAIRS GOING DOWN,A INNER VOICE TELLS YOU, AS
YOU GO DOWN YOU WILL GO INTO YOUR PAST. DO NOT
BE AFRAID,AT ANY TIME IF YOU CHOOSE TO LEAVE THEN
ALL YOU HAVE TO DO IS CLAP YOUR HANDS OR HIT
YOURSELF AND YOU WILL BE BACK HOME. YOU DECIDE

YOU ARE READY AND YOU GO DOWN THE STEPS, THEN YOU ARE IN A MOVIE THEATER, THE MOVIE IS ABOUT TO START. YOU LIKE MOVIES SO YOU ASK FOR YOUR FAVORITE DRINK AND SOME POPCORN. AS YOU ARE SETTING THEIR WAITING FOR THE MOVIE TO START YOU TASTE THE DRINK, IT IS COLD GOING DOWN. YOU TASTE THE BUTTER POPCORN. YOU ARE USING YOUR FIVE SENSES TO SEE, HEAR, TOUCH, SMELL AND TASTE. THE MOVIE STARTS THEIR IS A WOMAN HAVING A BABY, YOU LOOK AT THIS WOMAN AND REALIZE THIS IS YOUR MOTHER. IS SHE WHITE, BLACK, OR WHAT COLOR? HOW OLD DOES SHE LOOK? NOW YOU ARE BORN, WHAT DO YOU LOOK LIKE? REMEMBER YOUR PAST LIFE YOU CAN BE ANOTHER RACE, CULTURE, MALE OR FEMALE, RICH OR POOR. AS YOU WATCH THIS MOVIE AND SEE YOUR LIFE FLASH BEFORE YOU, NOTICE THE LITTLE THINGS. WHAT LANGUAGE DO THEY SPEAK? DO YOU HAVE ANY BROTHERS OR SISTERS? WHAT ARE THEIR NAMES? WHAT IS YOUR MOTHERS NAME? WHAT IS YOUR FATHERS NAME? WHAT IS YOUR NAME? SOMETINES YOU HAVE TO GO THRU THIS SEVERAL TIMES AND EACH TIME YOUR SUBCONSCIOUS WILL REVEAL A LITTLE MORE SO BE PATIENT. REMEMBER TO BE WILLING TO FACE SOME OF THE THINGS YOU MIGHT HAVE DONE AND HOW YOU DID DIE. HOW LONG DID YOU LIVE? DID YOU DO ANYTHING WITH YOUR PAST LIFE? DID YOU GET MARRIED? HAVE ANY CHILDREN? WHAT KIND OF WORK DID YOU DO? AFTER THE MOVIE IS OVER, REMEMBER YOU CAN ALWAYS OPEN THE DOOR AND GO UP THE STAIRS, OR IF YOU LOOK AROUND THEIR SHOULD BE ANOTHER DOOR THAT WILL LEAD DOWN TO ANOTHER LIFE. I HAVE LIVED OVER 2,000 YEARS SO I HAVE GONE THRU MANY DOORS. IN MY BOOKS AND POEMS I TRY TO WRITE SOME OF THE IMPORTANT THINGS I HAVE DONE. THIS IS GOOD THERAPY FOR ME AND NOW I KNOW A LITTLE ABOUT WHO I AM AND WHO I BEEN. I AM ALMOST 60 YEARS OLD NOW IN THIS TEMPORARY PHYSICAL BODY BUT YEARS MEAN NOTHING TO ME, ESPECIALLY SINCE

I HAVE LIVED OVER 2,000 YEARS.SO EVERY TIME I GO THRU THESE SIMPLE MEDITATIONS I CAN RECALL A LITTLE MORE OF EACH PAST LIFE, SOME I CHOOSE TO IGNORE BECAUSE IT DOES NOT HELP ME NOW. YES SOME OF MY PAST LIFE'S I CHOSE TO TAKE A SABBATICAL AND JUST REST. I CHOSE TO SIMPLY BE A NOBODY AND DO NOTHING FOR 60-80 YEARS. DOES THAT MAKE ME BAD? I AM A WATCHER, WHICH MEANS I GO THRU THE OUT OF BODY EXPERIENCE AND SEE WHAT OTHERS ARE DOING. IT IS NOT MY JOB TO TELL OTHERS WHAT THEY NEED TO DO WITH THEIR LIVES BUT IN TIMES I HAVE WENT INTO OTHER PHYSICAL BODIES TO WARN THEM OF WHAT THEY ARE ABOUT TO DO OR EXPECT. THE END RESULT IS STILL UP TO THEM. I MERELY TELL THEM WHEN THIS LIFE IS OVER THEY WILL HAVE TO STAND BEFORE OUR CREATORS. YES," EVERY KNEE SHALL BOW AND EVERY TONGUE SHALL CONFESS" AS THEIR WHOLE LIFE FLASHES BEFORE THEM.I CAN NOT STAND BEFORE GOD,GODDESS AND YAHSHUA,THIS IS SOMETHING YOU WILL DO AT THE END OF EACH PHYSICAL LIFE YOU LIVE. YOU CAN NOT BUY ENOUGH ANIMALS TO SACRIFICE FOR YOU AND NO PREACHER OR RABBI CAN HELP YOU. THEN YOU WILL SEE THAT WHAT I AM WRITING ABOUT WILL BE TRUE. YOU ARE ACCOUNTABLE AND RESPON-SIBLE FOR WHAT EVER SIN YOU COMMIT. SOMETIMES IT DOES TAKE TWO TO THREE LIFETIMES FOR JUSTICE TO HAPPEN. YAHSHUA WARNED US THOSE "WHO LIVED BY THE SWORD WILL DIE BY THE SWORD." BUT WHAT YAHSHUA DOES NOT TELL YOU IT MAY BE THREE LIFE-TIMES BEFORE YOU MAY BE DYING BY A SWORD OR KNIFE. KARMA HAS NO SENSE OF TIME.HOW DO YOU KNOW WHAT IT IS LIKE TO DIE BY FIRE UNLESS YOU ACTUALLY EXPERIENCE IT? HOW DO YOU KNOW WHAT IT IS LIKE TO FALL OFF A MOUNTAIN AND DIE UNLESS YOU ACTUALLY EXPERIENCE IT?HOW MUCH PAIN CAN A BODY ACCEPT? IT WOULD BE NICE IF EVERY DEATH WAS PAINLESS BUT WOULD YOU EXPERIENCE OR GROW IF EVERYTHING WAS PERFECT AND IN ORDER?. IF EV-

ERYLIFE WAS PERFECT AND YOU HAD NO ILLNESS, NO PAIN WOULD YOU EVER BE COMPLETELY HAPPY? IF WE GO THRU PAIN THEN WE EXPERIENCE THIS AND LEARN FROM OUR MISTAKES. IF YOUR FATHER TOLD YOU THAT A FIRE WOULD BURN YOU, WOULD YOU BE SATISFIED TO JUST SIMPLY TRUST HIM? MAYBE FOR AWHILE BUT SIMPLE HUMAN CURIOSITY WILL EVENTUALLY WANT TO KNOW TO EXPERIENCE THIS SO EVENTUALLY YOU WILL STICK YOUR FINGER IN THE FIRE TO SEE FOR YOUR SELF. DEEP DOWN WE ALL ARE A LOT LIKE DOUBTING THOMAS. DID GOD KNOW THAT EVENTUALLY ADAM AND EVE WOULD TASTE THIS FORBIDDEN FRUIT? YES OF COURSE. IF YOU HAVE KIDS OF YOUR OWN AND YOU TELL THEM TO NOT DO SOMETHING THAT IS RIGHT IN FRONT OF THEM LIKE A CERTAIN BOX,DO NOT OPEN IT UP. HOW LONG DO YOU THINK BEFORE THEY WILL HAVE TO TAKE A PEEK? KNOWING MY CHILDREN I GIVE THEM MAYBE 4 HOURS OR AS SOON AS I AM GONE. ITS PART OF OUR NATURE.

CHAPTER 9

THIS WILL BE THE NINTH CHAPTER,ARE WE UNDER THE LAW? IF YOU LIVE IN THE UNITED STATES THEN YOU REALIZE A LOT OF THE LAWS ARE NOT THE SAME AS GOD'S LAWS. FOR EXAMPLE,ACCORDING TO GOD'S LAW WHEN A BOY OR GIRL REACH THEIR 13TH BIRTH-DAY THEY GO THRU WHAT THE HEBREW/JEWISH CALL A BAR/BAT MITSVAH. THEY ARE NO LONGER CONSIDERED A BOY OR GIRL BUT A YOUNG MAN OR WOMAN. THEY HAVE GONE THRU THEIR 12 YEARS OF TRAINING AND ARE READY TO BE MARRIED,START TO WORK,USUALLY IN THEIR FATHERS PROFESSION AND HAVE CHILDREN OF THEIR OWN. IN THE PAST A MATCHMAKER WOULD ARRANGE THE MARRIAGE TO HELP UNIFY THE DIFFER-ENT TRIBES OR PEOPLE.REMEMBER WHEN JESUS/YAH-SHUA WAS ALIVE THEIR WAS NO CHRISTIAN CHURCH. THAT WAS NOT CREATED UNTIL AFTER HE DIED.

THEREFORE JESUS/YAHSHUA NEVER WORSHIPPED HIS FATHER ON SUNDAY BUT OBEYED ALL THE HEBREW/JEWISH CUSTOMS AND LAWS. ACCORDING TO THE LAW WHEN THE VIRGIN MARY BECAME OF AGE SHE WAS PROMISED TO JOSEPH. NOW JOSEPH WAS A LITTLE OLDER AND WAS MARRIED BEFORE BUT HIS WIFE DIED. HE DID HAVE CHILDREN,WHICH BECAME JESUS/YAHSHUA HALF BROTHERS AND SISTERS. NOW ACCORDING TO THE LAWS OF THE UNITED STATES IF A OLDER MAN HAD SEX WITH A YOUNG VIRGIN WHO WE KNOW WAS UNDER THE AGE OF 18 THEN HE WOULD GO TO JAIL, BE LABELED AS A SEXUAL PREDATOR, HAVE A FELONY ON HIS RECORD AND BE LABELED AND MARKED FOR THE REST OF HIS LIFE. DID JOSEPH BREAK GOD'S LAWS? NO DID JOSEPH BREAK THE LAWS OF THE UNITED STATES? ONLY IF HE LIVED HERE IN THE PRESENT TIME PERIOD. OBVIOUSLY HE WAS NOT UNDER OUR LAW. NOW WHAT ABOUT WHAT GOD DID? IF YOU READ IN DEUTERONO-MY CHAPTER 22 STARTING WITH VERSE 23,GO AHEAD AND STOP AND READ THIS.I KNOW YOU PROBABLY HAVE A BIBLE SOMEWHERE,DON'T YOU? NOW IF GOD LOOKED DOWN, SAW THIS VIRGIN WHO HE KNOWS WAS BETROTHED TO JOSEPH BUT TOLD JOSEPH NOT TO HAVE SEX WITH HER BECAUSE HE WANTED TO. JOSEPH HAD NO CHOICE BUT TO OBEY. A CHILD WAS BORN, JOSEPH KNEW THIS WAS NOT HIS SON BUT IN HONOR OF GOD HE RAISED HIM UP AS HIIS OWN. NOW ACCORDING TO THE LAWS OF THE UNITED STATES DID GOD CREATE A FELONY? OF COURSE. DO WE LABEL GOD AS A SEXUAL PREDATOR? NO, GOD IS NOT UNDER THE LAWS OF THE UNITED STATES BUT WHAT ABOUT HIS OWN LAWS? IF THIS WOMAN WAS A VIRGIN, PROMISED TO SOMEONE ELSE AND A MAN HAD SEX WITH HER THEN RAN OFF SHOULD THIS MAN BE STONED TO DEATH? YES, ACCORDING TO HEBREW/JEWISH LAW. DID GOD MARRY THIS VIRGIN MARY? NO, DID GOD PAY ANY CHILD SUPPORT? NO,SHOULD GOD BE STONED BY HIS OWN LAWS? DID GOD BREAK HIS OWN LAWS?

YOU DECIDE. WHAT DO YOU CALL A CHILD BORN OUT OF WEDLOCK? THIS IS WHY THE JEWISH,ISLAM AND OTHER RELIGIONS DO NOT ACCEPT JESUS/YAHSHUA AS THE SON OF GOD. THE CHOSEN PEOPLE DO NOT ACCEPT WHAT THEIR FATHER HAD DONE. THIS COULD NOT BE THE MESSIAH, THEY ARE STILL WAITING ON THEIR MESSIAH TO COME. THE ONLY GOOD THING THAT DID HAPPEN IS WHEN A JEWISH PERSON DOES COMMIT A SIN THEN THEY DO NOT HAVE TO FIND A CALF,SHEEP OR OTHER ANIMAL TO TAKE TO THE RABBI TO PAY FOR THEIR SINS. SO THE SACRIFICIAL LAW IS OVER.HOW DO THEY PAY FOR THEIR SINS? I DO NOT KNOW,I AM NOT JEWISH. I DO KNOW THAT I AM NOT SAVED BY GRACE. I AM RESPONSIBLE AND ACCOUNT-ABLE FOR ANY SIN I COMMIT AND I AM SURE EVERY PERSON,NO MATTER WHAT LABEL THEY WANT TO CALL THEMSELVES, EITHER JEWISH,ISLAM,HINDU,CHR ISTIAN,ETC IS ACCOUNTABLE AND RESPONSIBLE FOR WHAT EVER SIN THEY COMMIT. ITS NICE TO THINK WE CAN GO OUT AND DO WHAT EVER SIN WE WANT TO, DON'T WORRY ALL YOU HAVE TO DO IS RIGHT BEFORE YOU DIE ASK GOD TO FORGIVE YOU AND ALL YOUR SINS WILL BE INSTANTLY WASHED AWAY. IF YOU DON'T BELIEVE ME JUST GO TO ANY SO CALLED CHRIS-TIAN CHURCH, ON SUNDAY, PUT A HUNDRED DOLLAR BILL IN THE OFFERING PLATE WHEN THEY PASS IT AROUND,MAKE SURE THE PREACHER SEE'S YOU AND TELL HIM YOU WANT TO ASK FORGIVENESS, THEN YOU ARE INSTANTLY FORGIVEN WITH NO RESPONSIBLITY OR ACCOUNTABILITY. ITS AMAZING WHAT YOU CAN BUY FOR A HUNDRED DOLLARS TODAY.NOW IF YOU THINK OF THE HOLY SPIRIT AS THE FEMALE SIDE OF GOD THEN READ LUKE CHAPTER ONE THEN YOU WILL SEE THE HOLY SPIRIT,THE GODDESS WENT INTO THE VIRGIN FIRST. THEN,OUR FATHER GOD MERELY HAD SEX WITH HIS WIFE,USING THE VIRGIN MARY AS THE VESSEL TO DELIVER THIS CHILD. I OFTEN WONDER WHY GOD DID NOT JUST CREATE JESUS/YAHSHUA JUST

LIKE HE DID ADAM AND EVE? THE WORLD NEEDED TO KNOW THIS CHILD WAS BORN USING A VIRGIN AS A VESSEL AND THE "IMMACULATE CONCEPTION" PROVES THAT AFTER JESUS/YAHSHUA WAS BORN THEN THE VIRGIN MARY WAS PROVEN TO STILL BE A VIRGIN. GOD KEPT HIS PROMISE TO JOSEPH BY DELIVERING HIM A VIRGIN BRIDE. DID THEY HAVE OTHER CHILDREN? YES I DO BELIEVE,GOD TOLD US TO BE "FRUITFUL AND MULTIPLY". WAS JESUS/YAHSHUA MARRIED? YES I DO BELIEVE. ASK ANY HEBREW/JEWISH PERSON WHAT ARE THE STANDARD CUSTOMS TO BE A RABBI. MOST WILL SAY THEY HAVE TO BE MARRIED AND A SON BORN TO KEEP THEIR LINEAGE GOING. THAT WAS ONE OF THE CUSTOMS BACK THEN. REMEMBER THEIR WERE 12 TRIBES OF ISRAEL USUALLY THE LEVI TRIBE WAS THE PRIESTLY TRIBE. THE VIRGIN MARY,JOHN THE BAPTIST AND HER COUSIN ELIZABETH WERE ALL FROM THE LEVI TRIBE. JOSEPH WAS FROM THE TRIBE OF JUDAH WHICH EVERYONE KNEW THE MESSIAH WOULD COME. THE PEOPLE CALLED HIM RABBI WHY? DID JESUS/YAHSHUA GO THRU THE TRAINING TO BE A RABBI? YES HOW CAN YOU TELL THE DIFFERENCE FROM A PRIVATE IN THE ARMY AND A GENERAL? SAY THEY ARE BOTH WEARING THE SAME GREEN FATIGUE PANTS,SHIRT AND HAT? WHEN YOU WALK UP TO ONE HOW DO YOU KNOW WHAT RANK THEY ARE? THEY HAD LITTLE EMBLEMS EITHER STRIPES OR STARS ON THEIR SHOULDER OR COLLAR TO SHOW WHAT THEY HAVE EARNED. THE SAME WITH THE VARIOUS RANK OF ANY HEBREW/JEWISH PERSON, EITHER VARIOUS COLORS OF ROBES ARE DIFFERENT EMBLEMS ON THEIR BREASTPLATE, OR DIFFERENT COLOR BELTS THEY WRAPPED AROUND THEIR WAIST,KIND OF LIKE KARATE OR JUDO A ORANGE BELT,BROWN BELT AND A BLACK BELT TO SIGNIFY DIFFERENT DEGREE'S.

CHAPTER 10

THIS WILL BE THE TENTH CHAPTER, CHRISTIAN WICCA. SOME OF YOU HEARD AND OR READ THE BOOK CHRISTIAN WICCA BY NANCY CHANDLER PITTMAN. WHAT DO YOU THINK ABOUT IT? IF YOU HAVE NOT READ THE BOOK,THEN WHAT DO YOU THINK ABOUT COMBINING CHRISTIANITY WITH WICCA? A LOT OF WHAT SHE SAYS I WILL AGREE. I HAVE GONE THRU THE THREE WICCA INITIATIONS,"AND YOU HARM NONE,DO WHAT YOU WILL". NOW ALL RELIGIONS MAKE SENSE.IF YOU CAN IMAGINE,IN THE BEGINNING THERE WAS A MALE GOD AND A FEMALE GODDESS AND EVERYTHING WAS CREATED IN "OUR IMAGE,IN THE IMAGE OF US" THEN THE BIBLE MAKES SENSE.THE ONLY PROBLEM I HAVE WITH HER AND HER RELIGION IS SHE WANTS TO CREATE A NEW RELIGION,DOES SHE KEEP THE 7TH DAY SABBATH AS A TIME FOR REST? OR DOES SHE TRY TO FOLLOW THE

MAJORITY OF FALSE CHRISTIANS AND SAY ITS OK TO WORSHIP ON SUNDAY, THE FIRST DAY OF THE WEEK? DOES SHE TRY TO TEACH ABOUT THE CLEAN/UNCLEAN FOOD LAWS WICH ARE KOSHER? OR DOES SHE,LIKE THE MAJORITY OF FALSE CHRISTIANITY SAY ITS OK TO EAT WHAT EVER YOU WANT TO, WE ARE SAVED BY GRACE AND NOT UNDER THE "OLD LAW"? DOES SHE TEACH RE-INCARNATION? DOES SHE TEACH YOU ARE LIVING YOUR HEAVEN AND/OR HELL RIGHT NOW? DOES SHE TELL EVERYONE TO WASTE THIS 40,60,80 YEARS YOU ARE LIVING AND HOPEFULLY IF YOU BEEN A GOOD LITTLE BOY OR GIRL THEN WHEN YOU DIE YOU GET TO GO TO HEAVEN OR FOREVER BURN IN HELL FOREVER AND EVER? I DO ADMIRE HER FOR WHAT SHE HAS DONE AND THAT IS AT LEAST GUIDE US INTO THE RIGHT DIRECTION. SHE KNOWS THE FATHER GOD HAS TO HAVE A OPPOSITE AND THAT IS THE MOTHER WHICH ALWAYS HAS BEEN THE GODDESS, NO MATTER WHAT NAME YOU CALL HER. LOOK AT ALL THE CIVILIZATIONS THRU OUT HISTORY THAT BELIEVED IN A MALE/FEMALE FORMAT,EGYPTIAN,OSIRIS AND ISIS,ROMAN,JUPITER AND JUNO,GREEK,ZEUS AND HERA,CELTIC,CERRUNOS AND CERRIDWEN,TEUTONIC,ODIN AND FREYA AND DONT FORGET THE MAYAN OF MEXICO AND OUR OWN NORTH AMERICA INDIANS WHO SIMPLY CALLED HIM FATHER SKY AND MOTHER EARTH. HOW CAN SO MANY CIVILIZATIONS BELIEVE IN THIS EQUALITY FOR SO MANY THOUSANDS OF YEARS AND BE WRONG? THE FUNNY THING IS THAT IT TOOK A ROMAN EMPERIOR IN 313 AD BY THE NAME OF CONSTANTINE TO COMBINE THE OLD RELIGION WITH HIS VERSION OF A NEW RELIGION. I UNDERSTAND THE LOGIC AND NEED TO GET EVERYONE ON THE SAME PAGE. SOCIETY HAS BEEN TRYING TO GET EVERYONE UNDER ONE RELIGION,ONE GOVERNMENT,ONE LANGUAGE FOR THOUSANDS OF YEARS. HAVE THEY HAD MUCH SUCCESS? LOOK AROUND AT ALL THE DIFFERENT CHURCH'S AND DIFFERENT RELIGIONS,EITHER THE PEOPLE OR THE POWERS ABOVE

DO NOT WANT TO UNITE. THEY LIKE US TO BE "SCATTERED AND CONFUSED" ITS BETTER TO CONTROL US. DO YOU EVER WONDER WHY LUCIFER DID REBELL IN THE FIRST PLACE? I HAVE SAID SOME DIFFERENT REASONS THRU MY THREE BOOKS AND AS I GET OLDER IT SEEMS I GET A LITTLE WISER OR ON THE OTHER HAND MORE STUPID. DID THE WORLD HAVE ONE CHURCH AND ONE RELIGION IN THE BEGINNING? YES, IF YOU READ THE BIBLE IT ALSO SAYS THEIR WAS ONE LANGUAGE ALSO, I BELIEVE IT WAS THE ORIGINAL HEBREW LANGUAGE.IF YOU READ GENESIS CHAPTER SIX THEN WHO WERE THESE SONS OF GOD? COULD THEY BE A PART OF THE THIRD OF THE ANGELS THAT WERE CAST OUT OF HEAVEN? SURELY THEY COULD NOT BE A PART OF THE TWO THIRDS THAT STAYED UP THERE,COULD THEY? I HINTED AROUND THAT THE FIRST BORN SON,LUCIFER WAS HOPING THAT SOME DAY HE WOULD RULE SOMETHING AND AFTER THOUSANDS OF YEARS AND THE OLD MAN STILL NOT DYING THEN WHAT KIND OF FUTURE DID HE HAVE TO LOOK FORWARD TO? THEN ANOTHER SCENERO WOULD BE THAT LUCIFER DID FELL IN LOVE WITH EVE AND HAD SEX WITH HER INSTEAD OF GIVING HER A APPLE TO EAT. WE DO KNOW THAT GOD,THE FATHER WAS SO MAD THAT HE TURNED HIM INTO A UGLY SERPENT. IF EVE WAS PREGNANT WITH TWINS AND THE BOY,CAIN HAD THE SEED OF LUCIFER AND HIS TWIN SISTER HAD THE SEED OF ADAM,THEN THAT WOULD BE ONE REASON WHY CAIN KILLED ABEL AND GOD MARKED CAIN BY CHANGING HIS SKIN COLOR SO EVERYONE WOULD KNOW WHAT HE HAD DONE. I GREW UP AS A BAPTIST AND AS A CHILD THIS WAS HOW WE WERE TAUGHT THAT THIS IS WHY WE HAVE BLACK PEOPLE AND WHITE PEOPLE. FOR THOUSANDS OF YEARS THE BLACK PEOPLE WERE UNDER SLAVERY FOR THE SINS OF CAIN. ITS AMAZING THAT NOW, WE HAVE A LITTLE OVER ONE HUNDRED YEARS OF FREEDOM WHEN ABRAHAM LINCOLN FREED THE SLAVES. HAS ANY ONE EVER NOTICE HIS FIRST NAME?

COULD THIS NEW ABRAHAM BE A DECENDANT OF THE ORIGINAL ABRAHAM? IF YOU BELIEVE IN RE-INCARNATION THEN YES IT IS POSSIBLE. WHY WAS ABRAHAM LINCOLN SHOT? COULD THE EVIL POWER UNDER LUCIFER,WHO IS THE RULER OF THIS WORLD, NOT WANT THIS EQUALITY? COULD THE FATHER AND MOTHER STEP IN AND SAY THIS IS ENOUGH OF THIS SLAVERY,THEY HAVE PAID FOR THEIR SINS? SOME OF MY PAST LIVES I WAS BORN AND LIVED THE LIFE OF A SLAVE,IN EGYPT AND I WAS TAKEN,IN CHAINS OUT OF AFRICA,AND SOLD INTO SLAVERY. REMEMBER THE PILGRIMS CAME OVER ON THE MAYFOWER IN THE SIXTEENTH CENTURY,DID THEY BRING SLAVES TO TAKE CARE OF THE CROPS AND DO THE MAJORITY OF HARD LABOR? OF COURSE,FROM THE MIDDLE OF THE SIXTEENTH CENTURY UNTIL THE MIDDLE OF THE EIGHTENTH CENTURY,ABOUT TWO HUNDRED YEARS AMERICA USED SLAVES. WE WERE SUPPOSED TO BE "ONE NATION UNDER GOD WITH LIBERTY,JUSTICE FOR ALL " OR SO THE WRITERS WROTE ABOUT OUR INDEPENDANCE IN 1776 BUT WAS IT LIBERTY AND JUSTICE FOR ALL OR JUST LIBERTY AND JUSTICE FOR ALL WHITE MEN? OBVIOUSLY THE BLACK PEOPLE WERE STILL SLAVES FROM 1776 UNTIL 1886 OR A LITTLE LESS THEN A HUNDRED YEARS. WHY DID WE FIGHT OUR OWN CIVIL WAR ? THE NORTH VERSES THE SOUTH? BROTHER AGAINST BROTHER AND FATHER AGAINST SON. WE USED THE RELIGION OF SUNDAY WORSHIP CHRISTIANITY TO CONTROL THE PAGAN AND FEMALE GODDESS WORSHIP. LOOK AT WHAT OUR FORE-FATHERS DID DURING THE SIXTEEN HUNDRED "WITCH TRIALS" THIS IS AMERICA, THE LAND OF THE FREE,HOME OF THE BRAVE, LIBERTY JUSTICE FOR ALL WHAT ABOUT JUSTICE AND FREEDOM FOR ALL THE WITCHES THAT WERE BURNED? THRU OUT HISTORY SOCIETY HAS DONE A LOT OF EVIL THINGS UNDER THE DISQUISE OF CHRISTIANITY. WE ARE STILL DOING IT AND WILL NOT LEARN FROM OUR MISTAKES. THE BIBLE TALKS ABOUT THIS

WORLD COMING TO A END SOME DAY IN THE FUTURE. WE CALL IT THE RAPTURE. SOONER OR LATER OUR CRE- ATORS WILL GET TIRED OF TRYING TO CHANGE US AND JUST LET IT ALL END AND START OVER. THEN WE WILL BE ONE RELIGION,ONE CHURCH AND ONE LANGUAGE WILL THAT ONE LANGUAGE STILL BE THE ORIGINAL HEBREW? I BELIEVE SO THEN WHAT WILL THE ONE CHURCH,ONE RELIGION BE CALLED? DO WE DARE CALL IT BAPTIST? METHODIST?PENTACOSTAL?CATHOLIC? OR EVEN CHRISTIAN? DO WE CALL IT JEWISH?ISLAM?HINDU?BUDDAH,OR? WOULD WE BE CHRISTIAN WICCA? OR PAGAN? COULD WE BE SIMPLY SONS AND DAUGHTERS? DO WE CALL THIS A RELIGION OR CHURCH? DO WE KEEP THE 7TH DAY SABBATH OR SUNDAY OR WHAT DAY DO WE WORSHIPP? WHAT ABOUT EVERY DAY? CAN WE EAT ANYTHING WE WANT TO OR WILL THEIR STILL BE CLEAN/UNCLEAN ANIMALS,BIRDS AND FISH TO HELP KEEP THE WORLD CLEAN? I MEAN WHY DO WE HAVE UNCLEAN ANIMALS,BIRDS AND FISH FOR? DID OUR CREATORS KNOW THAT WE WOULD BE A WASTEFUL SOCIETY AND SLOWLY DESTROY THIS BEAU- TIFUL WORLD THAT THEY CREATED? SO THEY CREATED PIGS,ANTS,CATFISH,LOBSTER,VULTURE AND BUZZARD AND OTHER SCAVENGER'S TO HELP KEEP THIS WORLD CLEAN? WILL THIS WORLD EVER FIGURE OUT THAT IN THE BEGINNING WE HAD ONE CHURCH,ONE RELIGION AND ONE LANGUAGE AND ONE DAY WE WOULD GO BACK TO THAT ONE CHURCH,ONE RELIGION AND ONE LANGUAGE? ONE OF MY OTHER BOOKS AT THE TIME I WAS STILL UNDER THE IDEA THAT WE WOULD ALL DIE AND EVENTUALLY GET TO GO TO THIS HEAVEN SO IN MY MIND WHEN WE DID GET TO GO TO HEAVEN THEN YES WE WOULD ALL BE ONE CHURCH,ONE RELIGION AND WE ALL SPOKE ONE LANGUAGE WHICH I BELIEVED WOULD BE HEBREW. AS A BAPTIST WE USED TO SING THAT SONG " WHEN WE ALL GET TO HEAVEN,WHAT A DAY OF REJOICING THAT WILL BE. WHEN WE ALL SEE JESUS WE WILL SING AND SHOUT THE VICTORY" YES

BROTHERS AND SISTERS ONE DAY WE WILL ALL DIE AND GET TO GO TO HEAVEN, I WILL PASS THIS OFFERING PLATE AROUND AND IF YOU WANT TO GO TO HEAVEN THEN GIVE ME 10% OF YOUR MONEY OR MORE AND I,AS YOUR PREACHER WILL TALK TO GOD AND PUT IN A FEW GOOD WORDS FOR YOU. THOSE WHO PUT IN A LOT OF MONEY WILL GET A LOT OF WORDS PUT IN FOR THEM AND THOSE WHO ONLY GIVE A LITTLE WILL ONLY GET A FEW WORDS PUT IN. THE AMAZING THING IS PEOPLE ARE STILL FALLING FOR THIS LIE. THEY BELIEVE THIS PREACHER HAS THE POWER AND CONTROLS YOU. AS A NORMAL HUMAN BEING YOU CAN NOT GO DIRECTLY TO GOD,YOU HAVE TO GO THRU YOUR PREACHER,PRIEST OR RABBI. AS YOU READ THIS,WHERE DO YOU FIT IN? DO YOU EVEN GO TO A CHURCH? WHAT RELIGION DO YOU CALL YOUR SELF? WHAT DAY DO YOU WORSHIP THIS GOD? DOES IT MATTER? WHAT ABOUT THIS CHRISTIAN WICCA? CAN WE JOIN THE MALE AND FEMALE TOGETHER? DO WE CALL IT CHRISTIAN WICCA? WHAT ABOUT JEWISH WICCA? ISLAM WICCA? HINDU WICCA? BUDDAH WICCA? OR FILL IN THE BLANK WICCA? WHAT DID ADAM AND EVE CALL THEIR CHURCH? WHAT DID THEY CALL THEIR RELIGION? WHAT IS THE DIFFERENCE BETWEEN CHURCH AND RELIGION? WHAT WOULD BE THE HEBREW WORD? I CALL OUR GROUP BROKEN WING MINISTRY,WHY? BECAUSE OF OUR SINS OUR WINGS HAVE BEEN BROKEN,JUST LIKE THE SHEEP WHO KEEPS RUNNING AWAY THEN FINALLY THE SHEPHERD BREAKS THE SHEEP'S LEG SO HE WANT RUN ANYMORE. WHEN THE SHEEP CRIES OUT IN PAIN THEN THE SHEPHERD HEARS HIS VOICE AND CARRIES THE SHEEP. WE ARE THE SAME,WE RUN FROM GOD THEN ONLY AS A LAST RESORT WE CRY OUT TO OUR CREATORS,WHEN EVERYTHING ELSE FELLS AND EXPECT DELIVERANCE. SO WE WONDER WHY OUR "WINGS ARE BROKEN" WHY CAN'T WE JUST FLY UP TO HEAVEN AND BE WITH OUR FATHER GOD AND MOTHER GODDESS? WHY CAN'T WE BE WITH OUR JESUS(YAHSHUA)? CAN YOU IMAGINE MILLIONS OF

PEOPLE ALL WANTING TO BE IN HEAVEN AT THE SAME TIME? SO THIS WORLD WAS CREATED TO GIVE US OUR OWN VERSION OF HEAVEN,IN THE BEGINNING IT WAS BEAUTIFUL,WE HAD EVERYTHING WE WANTED, THEN WHAT HAPPENED? WE LET THE FALLEN ANGELS CONVINCE US AND LOOK AT WHAT WE HAVE CREATED? ITS EASY TO BLAME SOMEONE ELSE BUT IF YOU ARE ALIVE, BREATHING AND READING THIS THEN YOU ARE JUST AS GUILTY AS THE NEXT PERSON. ITS EASY TO POINT YOUR FINGER AT SOMEONE ELSE AND SAY THEY DID IT.ITS EASY TO ACT LIKE DOUBTING THOMAS AND SAY I DON'T BELIEVE ANYTHING YOU SAY UNLESS I CAN TOUCH IT. WHAT YOU DON'T KNOW,AS A VAMPIRE I CAN SENSE YOU READING THIS AND I HAVE BEEN ABSORBING YOUR POWER. AS A WATCHER I CAN SEE IF YOU WILL DO ANYTHING DIFFERENT,WILL YOU MAKE THE CHANGE TO BETTER YOUR SELF AND SOCIETY AS A WHOLE. REMEMBER THEIR ARE A LOT OF EYES WATCHING YOU. ITS EASY TO SAY IT DOES NOT MATTER AND I AM ONLY ONE PERSON,WHAT DIFFERENCE DOES THAT MAKE? IMAGINE IF EVERYONE IN THE WHOLE WORLD FELT THAT WAY? ITS LIKE THE DOMINO EFFECT YOU CAN HAVE A THOUSAND TIMES THOUSAND DOMINOES STANDING AND NOTHING WILL HAPPEN. ONLY WHEN ONE DOMINOE REACHES OUT AND TOUCHES THE NEXT DOMINOE THEN WE CAN RECIEVE THIS CHAIN REACTION. WHEN ONE DOMINOE DECIDES TO BE SOLID AND NOT MOVE LIKE THE MIGHTY OAK THEN THE EFFECT CAN STOP. EVERY ACTION HAS A OPPOSITE REACTION,CAUSE AND EFFECT. WHERE ARE YOU AT IN THIS DOMINOE GAME OF LIFE? WHAT IF YOU ARE LIVING IN HEAVEN RIGHT NOW? WHAT ARE YOU DOING WITH YOUR LIFE? NOW YOU KNOW THE TRUTH WILL YOU,AS A HUMAN DOMINOE, TOUCH SOMEONE ELSE BY TELLING THEM AND SHARING THIS SECRET? IT WILL NO LONGER BE A SECRET IF EVERYONE WILL TELL EVERYONE ELSE. THEN IMAGINE WHAT THIS WORLD COULD BE LIKE ONCE EVERYONE KNOWS THEY ARE IN THEIR HEAVEN AND THEY

HAVE THE POWER TO CREATE ANYTHING THEY WANT. SO YOU WANT PEARLY GATES? THEN WHAT IS KEEPING YOU FROM CREATING THEM? ARE YOU WAITING ON SOMEONE ELSE TO DO IT FOR YOU? WILL THEIR PEARLY GATES BE AS PRETTY AS YOURS? WHAT ABOUT YOUR MANSION? ARE YOU WAITING FOR SOMEONE ELSE TO CREATE THIS MANSION FOR YOU? DO THEY KNOW WHAT COLOR YOU WANT TO PAINT EACH ROOM? DO THEY KNOW WHAT STYLE AND COLOR CARPET,LIGHT FIXTURES,BATH ROOM TILES OR MARBLE? THE BEAUTI- FUL THIG ABOUT OUR HOUSE WE HAD IT CUSTOM BUILT,WE DECIDED WHAT COLOR WALLS,CARPET,MARB LE,CABINETS,LIGHT FIXTURES,OUTSIDE BRICK,ETC. IT IS OUR HOUSE CUSTOM BUILT THE WAY WE WANTED IT. SURE YOU CAN BUY A HOUSE ALREADY BUILT AND RE- PAINT IT OR CHANGE IT TO SUIT YOUR OWN PERSONAL NEEDS BUT THIS IS OUR HEAVEN AND WHILE WE ARE HERE IN THIS LIFETIME INSIDE THIS TEMPORARY HUMAN BODY WE MIGHT AS WELL ENJOY IT. WE DO NOT SET AROUND WAITING ON THIS GOVERNMENT OR SOMEONE ELSE TO GIVE US A FREE HANDOUT. WE DE- CIDED IF WE WANT ANYTHING THEN WE SHOULD GO OUT,WORK AND EARN IT. I CAN RESPECT ANYONE WHO WILL DO THAT. IT DOES NOT MATTER WHAT COLOR OF SKIN YOU ARE TEMPORARY STUCK IN. IT DOES NOT MATTER WHEATHER YOU ARE MALE OR FEMALE DURING THIS LIFETIME. WHAT DOES MATTER IS YOU ACCEPT WHO YOU ARE NOW AND TRY TO DO WHAT YOU CAN TO EXPERIENCE THE THINGS YOU NEED TO DO NOW,AND NOT SET AROUND WITH YOUR HAND OUT WANTING SOMEONE ELSE TO TAKE CARE OF YOU. RE- MEMBER WHEN YOU DIE,YOUR SPIRIT/SOUL WILL LEAVE THIS PHYSICAL BODY AND YOU WILL GO TO THEIR HEAVEN AND BE JUDGED FOR WHAT ALL YOU DID DURING THIS LIFETIME. DID YOU ACCOMPLISH EVERY- THING? HAVE YOU EXPERIENCED EVERYTHING? DO YOU KNOW WHAT ITS LIKE TO EXPERIENCE EVERY PAIN? EVERY DISEASE? EVERY ILLNESS? HAVE YOU EXPERI-

ENCED BE RICH? WHAT DID YOU DO WITH YOUR
MONEY? HAVE YOU EXPERIENCED BE HOMELESS? WHY
DO WE HAVE GAY AND LESBIANS? DO WE NEED TO EXPE-
RIENCE THESE THINGS? I KNOW IN MY PAST BOOKS WE
THOUGHT OF THAT AS A ABOMINATION AGAINST GOD,
LOOK AT WHAT HAPPENED TO SODAM AND GOMAR-
RAH? NOW I REALIZE MAYBE WE NEED TO BE OUT OF
HORMONE BALANCE TO EXPERIENCE WHAT ITS LIKE.
TO ME EVERY PERSON HAS BOTH MALE AND FEMALE
HORMONE INSIDE THEM. AS I SAID BEFORE THE
NORMAL   MALE   WOULD   BE   80%   MALE
HORMONE,TESTOSTERONE AND ABOUT 20% FEMALE
HORMONE,ESTROGEN AS A SOLID BALANCE. THIS SEEMS
FAIR.THE AVERAGE HUMAN WOULD ALSO HAVE GOOD
AND EVIL INSIDE THIS IS A BALANCE AND IS UP TO YOU
WHICH ONE YOU FEED THE MOST. THE SAME WOULD
BE FOR A NORMAL FEMALE WITH 80% ESTROGEN AS
HER FEMALE HORMONE AND AROUND 20% TESTOSTER-
ONE TO GIVE HER A BALANCE. SOME HOW OR ANOTH-
ER THIS 80/20 BALANCE GOT OUT OF CONTOL. WE
TALKED ABOUT THIS BEFORE BUT BEARS REPEATING
AGAIN. I DO KNOW SOME PEOPLE WHO ARE LESBIAN
WHO SAY THEY ARE MALE TRAPPED IN A WOMANS BODY
OR GAY FRIENDS WHO SAY I AM A FEMALE TRAPPED
INSIDE THIS MALE BODY. SO YOU DECIDE IF THIS COULD
BE ANOTHER FORM OF RE-INCARNATION? I SAID IN ONE
OF MY PAST BOOKS THAT IF YOU TAKE OFF ALL YOUR
CLOTHES AND LOOK IN THE MIRROR AND SEE A MAN
THEN YOU NEED TO ACT LIKE A MAN. AT THE TIME I
SAID THAT I WAS VERY SINCERE IN MY NARROW BELIEF.
NOW I REALIZE I OWE SOME PEOPLE A APOLOGY. I ASK
THAT THEY WOULD ACCEPT THIS AS A APOLOGY FOR
MY IGNORANCE,WE HAVE A LOT OF SO CALLED CHRIS-
TIANS AND OTHERS WHO ARE STILL NARROW MINDED.
I CAN NOT APOLOGIZE FOR THEM BUT HOPE SOME
WOULD READ THIS AND UNDERSTAND WHY SOME
PEOPLE DO WHAT THEY DO AND ACT THE WAY THEY
DO. I HAVE NO RIGHT TO JUDGE THEM AND CAN ONLY

HOPE THEY ARE GOING THRU THIS EXPERIENCE AS A STEP UP THE CIRCULAR STAIRS. WHAT STEP ARE YOU ON NOW? WHAT DO YOU NEED TO EXPERIENCE NOW DURING THIS LIFE TO MOVE UP ANOTHER STEP? MY PRAYERS ARE TO MY FATHER GOD AND MOTHER GODDESS TO HELP ME TO HELP YOU GO UP THESE STEPS. AS YOU GO UP THESE STEPS THEN SO DO I, AS YOU READ THIS BOOK I HOPED I OPENED SOME DOORS,I ASKED A LOT OF QUESTIONS AND REALIZE THAT AFTER ALMOST SIXTY YEARS IN THIS LIFE AND TWO THOUSAND YEARS IN PREVIOUS LIVES I STILL HAVE A LOT TO LEARN AND EXPERIENCE. I LOVE BEING A VAMPIRE,I HAVE LEARNED TO NOT ONLY TAKE POWER AND ENERGY FROM PEOPLE BUT TO GIVE IT BACK. I CAN SENSE THE EVIL IN SOME PEOPLE,I ABSORB ALL I CAN FROM THEM,FILTER THIS EVIL ENERGY AND MAKE IT GOOD ENERGY AND THEN GIVE IT TO SOMEONE IN NEED.THIS IS ONE OF THE REASONS I AM HERE.WE ALL ARE LOOKING FOR THIS HARMONY. WE WILL NEVER HAVE HARMONY UNTIL WE HAVE EQUALITY AND WE WILL NEVER HAVE EQUALITY UNTIL WE HAVE BALANCE. ONCE WE REALIZE WE HAVE BOTH MALE AND FEMALE, GOOD AND EVIL INSIDE OF US AND WE ARE IN CONTROL. THE POWER WE DECIDE TO FEED THE MOST WILL BE THE POWER THAT DECIDED HOW WE ARE AND WHAT WE BECOME. REMEMBER YOU ARE ONLY STUCK IN THIS HUMAN BODY TEMPORARY,YOU ARE A IMMORTAL SPIRIT/SOUL WHO HAS LIVED MANY LIFETIMES.YOU ARE HERE TO EXPERIENCE CERTAIN THINGS.EVERYONE IS DIFFERENT,EVERYONE HAS LIVED DIFFERENT LIFETIMES,EVERYONE HAS A DIFFERENT FINGERPRINT BUT I BELIEVE YOU HAVE THE SAME FINGERPRINT IN YOUR PAST LIFE THAT YOU HAVE NOW. IN TIME SOCIETY WILL KEEP A RECORD OF ALL FINGERPRINTS AND NOT DELETE THEM WHEN SOMEONE DIES, THIS WAY YOU CAN VERIFY WHO YOU WAS IN A PAST LIFE. ALSO REMEMBER ONE LIFE YOU MAY BE BORN IN AMERICA AND THE PAST LIFE OR NEXT LIFE YOU COULD BE BORN

IN CHINA OR AFRICA,ETC. REMEMBER THOSE WHO YOU HATE DURING THIS LIFE YOU MAYBE IN YOUR NEXT LIFE. FOR EXAMPLE THIS LIFE YOU MAY BE A CHRISTIAN AND YOUR NEXT LIFE MAYBE ISLAM BUT DON'T EXPECT 20 VIRGINS BECAUSE YOU MAY BE ONE OF THESE 20,RE-MEMBER "YOU REAP WHAT YOU SOW" . TO END THIS BOOK I SAY AS A CHRISTIAN IN THIS LIFE I PRAY IN JESUS(YAHSHUA) NAME AMEN AND SHALOM I PRAY FOR PEACE IN AMERICA. I PRAY FOR PEACE IN ISRAEL AND ALL THE WORLD I PRAY THAT IF IT IS OUR GOD AND GODDESS WILL THAT PEOPLE WILL READ THIS BOOK.

CHAPTER 11

NOW WE COME TO CHAPTER ELEVEN. WHAT I WILL CALL THE SYNOPIS. MY OTHER BOOKS I DIVIDED INTO 14 CHAPTERS, SO WHY ONLY ELEVEN THIS TIME? I DON'T HAVE AS MUCH TO SAY AND A LOT OF WHAT I DID SAY I REPEATED OVER AND OVER AGAIN. I ALSO REALIZED AS I PROOFREAD EACH CHAPTER I REALIZED I SPELLED A FEW WORDS WRONG AND DID NOT DO GOOD GRAMMAR. I HAD THE OPPORTUNITY TO CHANGE THIS BUT AGAIN THAT LITTLE VOICE TOLD ME TO LEAVE IT ALONE. THIS WAY PEOPLE WILL KNOW THAT YOU ARE HUMAN AND DO MAKE MISTAKES. MY OTHER TWO BOOKS I PUT EVERY LETTER OF EVERY WORD AS CAPITAL LETTERS. SO WHY DID I NOT DO THIS BOOK THE SAME WAY? I HAVE NOTHING TO GAIN TO PROVE THAT I AM A REBEL. IF YOU HAVE NOT FIGURED THAT OUT BY NOW THEN IT WILL NOT HAPPEN. I DO APOLOGIZE FOR

REPEATING OVER AND OVER,LIKE A BROKEN RECORD SOME OF THE TOPICS I DISCUSSED,AGAIN I WANTED THE AVERAGE READER TO UNDERSTAND,THRU REPETITIONS,THE MAIN TOPIC I WAS TRYING TO GET ACROSS. IF YOU WANT TO LABEL ME AS CRAZY,THAT IS YOUR CHOICE. MAYBE I AM CRAZY,ARE WE ALL ARE A LITTLE BIT CRAZY? IF YOU IMAGINE THIS LIFE YOU ARE LIVING RIGHT NOW,EVERYONE IS PLAYING THE GAME OF HIDE AND GO SEEK. YOU CLOSE YOUR EYES AND COUNT TO TWENTY,BUT WHEN YOU OPEN THEM,EVERYONE IS STANDING AT THE SAME PLACE. NO ONE IS HIDING. IS THIS A FUN GAME? IMAGINE YOU BUY THIS PUZZLE WITH A 1,000 PIECES IN IT AND YOU LOOK FORWARD TO EVERY DAY PUTTING A NEW PIECE OF THIS PUZZLE CALLED LIFE.THEN YOU WAKE UP THE NEXT DAY,ALL EXCITED ABOUT PUTTING THE FIRST PIECE,ONLY TO FIND THE PUZZLE IS ALREADY COM-PLETELY PUT TOGETHER? WHERE IS THE FUN? WHERE IS THE EXCITEMENT? WOULD LIFE BE A LITTLE BORING IF OUR PUZZLE WAS ALREADY PUT TOGETHER? WOULD OUR LIFE BE A LITTLE BORING IF WE OPEN OUR EYES AND EVERYONE IS JUST STANDING THERE? HOW DO YOU PLAY YOUR GAME CALLED LIFE? DO YOU JUST SET AROUND AND WAIT TO DIE? HOPING THAT ALL THE RE-LIGIONS ARE TRUE AND WHEN YOU DO FINALLY DIE GET TO GO TO THIS PLACE CALLED HEAVEN? OR WAS YOU A BAD LITTLE GIRL OR BOY AND SANTA CLAUS IS NOT BRINGING YOU NO PRESENT AND YOU WILL SPEND ALL OF ETERNITY BURNING IN THIS PROVERBIAL PLACE CALLED HELL? AS YOU GO THRU THIS LIFE ARE THERE ONLY TWO CHOICES? ARE THERE ONLY TWO JOBS YOU CAN WORK AT? ARE THERE ONLY TWO WOMAN YOU CAN MARRY? ARE THERE ONLY TWO HOUSES YOU CAN LIVE IN? CAN YOU ONLY HAVE TWO CHILDREN,ONE HAS TO BE A BOY AND THE OTHER HAS TO BE A GIRL? I COULD GO ON AND ON WITH THIS SCENERO BUT YOU UNDERSTAND WHAT I AM GETTING AT. SO WHY DO YOU,AT THE END OF THIS LIFE, ONLY HAVE TWO CHOIC-

ES? YOU WILL STAND BEFORE YOUR CREATORS,EVERY KNEE SHALL BOW AND EVERY TONGUE SHALL CONFESS. IF OUR GOD/GODDESS WERE FAIR THEN EVERY PERSON COULD NOT BE JUDGED THE SAME BECAUSE EVERY PERSON DONE DIFFERENT CRIMES.WHEN YOU GO BEFORE A TRIAL AND JURY FOR A CRIME YOU COMMIT-ED IS THERE ONLY TWO CHOICES? WILL THE JURY AND JUDGE SENTENCE EVERYONE TO THE SAME SENTENCE NO MATTER WHAT THE CRIME IS? OF COURSE NOT. SO IF A JUDGE HERE ON EARTH SENTENCED YOU TO A CER-TAIN TIME OR PUNISHMENT ACCORDING TO THE CRIME COMMITED,WOULD NOT OUR HEAVENLY JUDGE'S DO THE SAME? THERE ARE SOME CHURCH'S THAT DO BELIEVE IN THIS FUTURE RAPTURE,THAT ONE DAY JESUS(YAHSHUA) WILL RETURN IN THE SKY, "THE GRAVES WILL GIVE UP THE DEAD,THE SEAS WILL GIVE UP THE DEAD AND THOSE THAT ARE ALIVE WILL BE CAUGHT UP AND GET TO GO TO HEAVEN." DOES THIS MAKE SENSE? IF ADAM DIED THOUSANDS OF YEARS AGO THEN HOW CAN HE COME BACK ALIVE? DOES THE BIBLE NOT SAY FLESH AND BLOOD CAN NOT ENTER HEAVEN? TO ME THAT MEANS ONLY A SPIRIT/SOUL CAN ENTER HEAVEN TO BE JUDGED. SO WHO IS RIGHT? HALF THE CHURCH'S BELIEVE THE MOMENT YOU DIE YOU ARE IN HEAVEN AND THE OTHER HALF BELIEVE YOU ARE STILL IN THE GROUND? WHAT IF BOTH ARE RIGHT? WHAT IF THE MOMENT YOU DIE,YOUR FLESH AND BLOOD HUMAN BODY DOES GO BACK TO THE EARTH,FROM WHICH IT CAME. YOUR SPIRIT/SOUL DOES GO TO HEAVEN AND IS JUDGED ACCORDING TO WHAT IT DID DURING THIS LIFETIME. THEN YOU ARE RE-INCARNAT-ED INTO YOUR NEXT LIFE. THEN HOW WILL THE RAP-TURE WORK? IF THE SEAS WILL GIVE UP THE DEAD AND THE GRAVES GIVE UP THE DEAD? WE KNOW FOR A FACT THAT SOME PEOPLE,WHEN THEY DIE, ARE NOT READY TO GO TO THE LIGHT AND BE JUDGED.IN THE OTHER-WORLD, TIME MEANS NOTHING. ONE DAY IN THE OTHER WORLD COULD BE EQUAL TO A HUNDRED YEARS

ON THIS WORLD.WE DO KNOW WE HAVE GHOSTS AND SPIRITS HANGING AROUND.IF YOU READ THE BIBLE THEN YOU KNOW THAT JESUS(YAHSHUA) CAST OUT EVIL SPIRITS OUT OF CERTAIN PEOPLE. SO DO ONLY EVIL SPIRITS GET TO HANG AROUND FOR AWHILE? COULD GOOD SPIRITS HANG AROUND? DO WE HAVE THIS GUARDIAN ANGEL WATCH OVER US? COULD THERE BE TWO ANGELS WATCHING OVER US? ONE GOOD AND ONE EVIL? WHAT ABOUT THIS SPLIT PER-SONALITY? THIS DOCTOR JEKYLL AND MISTER HYDE EFFECT? IS THIS ALL DELUSIONAL? SCIENTIST,ATHEIST,EVOLUTIONIST AND DOCTORS CAN AGREE THAT SOME PEOPLE HAVE THIS PROBLEM WITH MANY PERSONALITIES. THE EVOLUTIONIST AND ATHI-EST CAN TAKE EVERY THING AND BREAK IT DOWN TO A SIMPLE ONE CELL.WHEN YOU ASK THEM WHERE THIS ONE CELL CAME FROM THEY CAN NOT EXPAIN IT. THEY ONLY KNOW THIS ONE CELL STARTED MULTIPLY-ING AND BECAME TWO CELLS,THEN FOUR CELLS, THEN EIGHT CELLS,THEN SIXTEEN CELLS,THEN THIRTY TWO CELLS,ETC.WE KNOW THAT EVERYTHING HAS MOLE-CULES WHICH CONSIST OF ATOMS WHICH CONSIST OF PROTRONS,ELECTRONS AND NEUTRONS. ALL YOUR EVOLUTIONIST CAN BREAK DOWN EVERYTHING FROM THIS ONE CELL BUT ASK THEM WHERE THIS ONE CELL CAME FROM AND THEY DO NOT HAVE A ANSWER. ITS LIKE THE "ONE HAND CLAPPING THEORY" IF YOU ONLY HAVE ONE HAND CAN IT MAKE A NOISE? IF YOU HAVE EVERYTHING IN LIFE THAT STARTED AS A "BIG BANG THEORY" THEN DOES IT TAKE TWO OF SOMETHING TO MAKE A BIG BANG? THEN WHERE DID THESE TWO THINGS COME FROM? AGAIN I ASK YOU WHERE DID THIS ONE CELL COME FROM? ONE THEORY WAS IT AT-TACHED TO A CRYSTAL,BUT THEN WHERE DID THE CRYSTAL COME FROM? THE BOTTOM LINE IS ALL THE EVOLUTIONIST AND ATHEIST ARE TRYING TO EXPLAIN THAT EVERYTHING COULD BE CREATED WITH OUT THIS GOD/GODDESS. THE FUNNY STORY GOES LIKE

THIS. A SCIENTIST FINALLY FIGURED OUT HOW TO CREATE LIFE SO HE CHALLENGED GOD TO A TEST. TO HUMOR HIM GOD ACCEPTS THE CHALLENGE. THE SCIENTIST SAYS HE HAS THE POWER TO CREATE LIFE AND BENDS OVER TO PICK UP A HAND FUL OF DIRT TO START HIS PROJECT. "WAIT" SAID GOD "THAT IS MY DIRT GO GET YOUR OWN DIRT" DID THIS SCIENTIST CREATE THIS DIRT? DID THIS SCIENTIST CREATE THIS WORLD? DID THIS SCIENTIST CREATE THIS ONE CELL? I HAVE NO PROBLEM UNDERSTANDING THAT LIFE STARTED OFF AS ONE CELL. IT WAS SIMPLY CALLED A MALE SPERM CELL,COULD IT CREATE LIFE BY IT SELF?NO THIS MALE SPERM CELL HAD TO SWIM AROUND IN SEARCH OF A FEMALE EGG CELL,THEN UNDER THE RIGHT CIRCUM-STANCE COULD THEY UNITE AND THE TWO CELLS START MULTIPLY-ING AND BECOME FOUR CELLS,THEN EIGHT CELLS,THEN SIXTEEN CELLS,THEN THIRTY TWO CELLS,ETC. THE EVOLUTIONIST IS PARTLY RIGHT BY SAYING LIFE STARTS OUT IN A OCEAN, THE OCEAN IS THE WATER INSIDE THE WOMB,THE UMBILICAL CORD IS THE LIFELINE THAT FEEDS THIS BABY WHETHER IT IS A HUMAN BABY,A HORSE,COW,WHALE,FISH,BIRD,ANIM AL OR WHATEVER. DOES IT NOT AMAZE YOU THAT WE ALL HAVE THE SAME POWER TO CREATE LIFE JUST LIKE OUR CREATORS DID? IT DOES NOT MATTER WHETHER YOU ARE HUMAN, A BIRD,A ANIMAL OR A FISH. WHAT COMMON THREAD DO WE ALL HAVE TOGETHER? ARE WE ALL IN THE IMAGE OF "OUR " CREATORS. ARE WE ALL VAMPIRES AND NOT KNOW IT? ARE WE ALL EITHER A PREDATOR OR A VICTIM IN THIS GAME CALLED LIFE? ONE THING YOU DO KNOW IS "YOU WANT GET OUT OF THIS WORLD ALIVE" YOU CAME ITO THIS WORLD,NAKED AND WITH NOTHING AND YOU WILL LEAVE THIS WORLD WITH NOTHING,SURE THOUSANDS OF PEOPLE HAVE TRIED TO TAKE VALUABLES WITH THEM. ONLY TO REAL-IZE THEY DO NOT OWN ANYTHING THEY ARE ONLY TEMPORARY STEWARDS. WHAT GOLD,SILVER DIA-MONDS DO YOU OWN? OR THINK YOU OWN? ITS NICE

TO HAND DOWN VALUABLES TO YOUR HEIRS, WHETHER IT BE YOUR CHILDREN OR A GOOD CAUSE. IT WILL NOT BE YOUR PROBLEM WHAT THEY DO WITH IT, THEY WILL STAND COME JUDGEMENT DAY. SO COULD THIS RAPTURE STILL COME IN THE FUTURE? OF COURSE ANYTHINGISPOSSIBLE.SOMEPEOPLETHINKJESUS(YAHSHUA) WILL RETURN, WHY? WILL THIS WORLD FINALLY END? WILL ANY SURVIVE? DO WE HAVE A NEW ADAM AND EVE? WILL THEIR SKIN COLOR BE WHITE OR BLACK OR?? WHAT LANGUAGE WILL THEY SPEAK? WILL IT BE THE OLD HEBREW? WILL THERE BE THIS CHOICE OF "GOOD AND EVIL"? WILL WE BE CAST OUT OF THE GARDEN OF EDEN AGAIN AND AGAIN UNTIL WE LEARN TO OBEY? HOW MANY LIFETIMES DO WE HAVE TO LIVE TO EXPERIENCE ALL THE THINGS WE NEED TO EXPERIENCE? WHAT STEP ARE YOU ON, UNDER THIS STAIRCASE CALLED LIFE? IF YOU COULD LIVE LIFE OVER WHAT WOULD YOU CHANGE? DOES THIS BOOK MAKE ANY SENSE? DID YOU GET YOUR MONEY OUT OF IT? WILL YOU, NOW BECOME A DIFFERENT PERSON THEN BEFORE YOU READ THIS BOOK? WE ARE THE PROPHETS, WE ARE THE VAMPYRES, WE ARE THE WATCHERS. THIS IS THE CHRONICLES. THIS IS YOUR HEAVEN AND OR HELL, WHAT ARE YOU GOING TO DO ABOUT IT? SHALOM